The Rediscovery of Greece

Louis Dupré, *The House of the French Consul in Athens*, 1819

with 173 illustrations, 30 in colour

Fani-Maria Tsigakou

The Rediscovery of Greece

TRAVELLERS AND PAINTERS OF THE ROMANTIC ERA

Introduction by Sir Steven Runciman

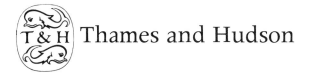 Thames and Hudson

To Mina

Text and monochrome illustrations printed in Great Britain by BAS Printers Ltd, Over Wallop,
Hampshire
Colour illustrations printed in Great Britain by Balding & Mansell Ltd, Wisbech, Cambs.
Bound in Great Britain by Webb Son & Co Ltd, Glamorgan

Contents

Acknowledgments

I would like to thank the Benaki Museum, Athens, and the Museum of the City of Athens for allowing me to draw extensively from their collections for my pictorial material. I would also like to acknowledge the permissions given by the following institutions to reproduce works of art in their collections: Gennadeios Library, National Gallery, National Historical Museum, Athens; Groeningemuseum, Bruges; Fitzwilliam Museum, Cambridge; Dick Institute, Kilmarnock; British Museum, Royal Institute of British Architects, Tate Gallery, Witt Library, London; Bayerische Staatsgemäldesammlungen, Staatliche Graphische Sammlung, Munich; Ashmolean Museum, Oxford; Bibliothèque Nationale et Universitaire, Strasbourg; Museo d'Arte Moderna Ca' Pesaro, Venice; Schweizerisches Landesmuseum, Zürich. Special thanks are also due to all those private collectors who kindly allowed me to reproduce works in their possession, particularly Georges Kouremetis and Mike Krassakis. I owe a special debt to the Fine Art Society, London, for their assistance and genuine enthusiasm for the project. All works in Greek collections have been photographed by Tassos Nollas.

I wish to record my gratitude to Professor and Xenia White for their concern and encouragement, and to Dr Angeliki Kokkou, Dr Miltos Papanikolaou, Mrs Angeliki Amandry, Mr Stathis Finopoulos, Miss Leonora Navarri and Professor Panos Tzonos who helped my work in various ways. My deepest gratitude goes to Colston Sanger for the numerous discussions we have had and for his timely criticism of the structure of the text. Finally, I have learned much from Nikos Stangos's painstaking reading and editing of my original typescript.

But most of all, I am indebted to Sir Steven Runciman for sharing this book with a student of his vast scholarship of all things Greek.

Fani-Maria Tsigakou   Athens, 1981

Introduction by Sir Steven Runciman

THE MUSE OF HISTORY needs her handmaidens. Her business is to tell a story; but the story will be meaningless if it is a mere chronicle of past events. We must try to find out how people in bygone ages lived, what were their material requirements and desires, what they saw about them, what they thought and felt, and what they created. History must have its illustrators; and none of them are more useful than the actual illustrators of the time, the artists. There have always been great artists far ahead of their times, whose work has had to wait for due appreciation. But the ordinary artist has his living to make. He must satisfy his clients. He must produce work that will arouse their interest and admiration. So, if we want to understand how our ancestors felt about some foreign land, it is from the artists who went there that we receive the clearest answers. The travel-writers are useful; for they too are descriptive artists in their way, with words instead of form and colour. But they are longer-winded, travelling sometimes for some special purpose or else to escape from contemporary life. They reflect less truly the spirit of the age.

The attitude of Western Europe towards Greece has gone through many changes. In the Middle Ages the Greeks were objects of ignorant suspicion and dislike, though their land was considered fair enough. Then in the wake of the Renaissance there came a growing admiration for ancient Greek literature and learning, though ancient Greek art was little known except from Roman copies and was not clearly differentiated from the Roman. Greek medieval art, which had impressed the medieval West, was now despised; and Greek lands were in infidel hands, and few Westerners other than merchants and diplomats found their way there. The interest was purely intellectual. Artists were only interested in Greece because its mythology supplied subjects for their canvases. It is true that the Western Churches kept an interest in the fate of the Eastern Christians. Rome sent Jesuits to work there, in the hope of capturing the Orthodox communities. The Protestants saw in the Orthodox allies against Rome. The Lutherans in the sixteenth and the Calvinists in the early seventeenth century flirted ineffectually with the Greek Patriarchate; and in the later seventeenth century the Church of England and the Non-Jurors wooed it for several decades, the only outcome being the ephemeral establishment of a Greek College at Oxford and the introduction of coffee-drinking into English polite society.

There was, however, a growing interest in classical antiquities. By the eighteenth century the rich in the West were beginning to collect them (and, travel being easier now, were ready to send out agents to discover and remove them), or went out themselves to indulge in a little destructive archaeology. In England the pioneers were the group of young noblemen who formed the Society of Dilettanti. But the dominant figure of the age was the German, Johann Joachim Winckelmann, who was the true founder of the study of Greek antiquities and who gave to classical Greek art the aesthetic pre-eminence which it has never since lost.

These expeditions always included an artist, to depict the monuments and the ruins, and sometimes, also, the sorry state of the great cities of the past. Contemporary Greece was of little interest to them. It was a land of poverty and squalor, full of thieves and superstitious clergy, dominated by corrupt if courteous Turks.

There followed the Romantic Movement and Lord Byron. Foreign lands were now enveloped with romance and native peoples were to be admired. The Greeks could not perhaps qualify as Noble Savages; but they soon acquired greater romantic glory with their struggle for independence. They were seen as being more or less the heirs of the antique Grecian world, classical figures in a classical landscape. But amongst the Philhellenes who came to fight in the war for freedom, or in its wake, were many who were entranced by the land of Greece itself. The earlier eighteenth-century dislike for rugged scenery had been dissipated by the Romantics; and now the sheer beauty of Greece was discovered. In the decades that followed landscape artists arrived to practice their art in Greece, especially from Britain, with Edward Lear as the most delightful of all.

To have this story told to us with wisdom, learning and sensibility and to have it amply and superbly illustrated is a pleasure for which all who read this book will be deeply grateful. It is a great privilege to be asked to introduce it.

I · The rediscovery of Greece

'So there is Greece! For her I have crossed this vast expanse of sea, abandoned Italy, my parents and my friends; all for this land! And why could I not make this journey in my own study, like the author of the young Anacharsis? Could I not have read the ancient and modern travellers, and learned painlessly about all that Greece holds in our own day, and about what existed there in olden times? Yes . . ., I could have done; but then I wanted to make it in order to feel. . . . What does it matter that Sparta, Athens and Corinth are gone for ever? The soil where they stood still holds in its breast the sublime ideas that it inspired in ancient times . . . And the silence! It will allow me to be moved and to breathe freely in this majestic theatre where so many glorious deeds were done.'

Saverio Scrofani, *Viaggio in Grecia*, 1799

The classical prelude

'GENTLEMEN, these stones, thanks to Phidias, Praxiteles, Agoracritus and Myron, are more precious than diamonds or agates: it is to these stones that we owe our political renaissance.' The speaker was the Greek scholar I. Rizos-Neroulos, and it was with these words that he opened the first conference of the Greek Archaeological Society in 1838 on the ancient acropolis of Athens.[1]

Opposite
Giovanni Battista Lusieri, *The Monument of Philopappus*, 1800

The connection made by Rizos-Neroulos between the achievements of classical Hellas and the emergence of the modern Greek state is characteristic: the emphasis on the example of the ancient Hellenes was to determine the ideological and cultural orientation of modern Greece. This was, indeed, how modern Greece was originally viewed throughout Europe: as a reflection of the idea of ancient Hellas. Classical studies in the West from the Renaissance onwards, together with a more generalized, nostalgic vision of ancient Greece, had played a fundamental role in the creation of the modern Greek state. The new Greece that was created in 1828, after the country had won its independence from Ottoman rule, was, moreover, modelled by its European guarantors rather than by the Greeks themselves.

The idea of ancient Greece has had a profound and reverberating influence on the West: it was, indeed, a vision that manifested itself in different ways at different times. To most Europeans before the sixteenth century – but also later – Greece possessed an identity entirely in terms of its past. The country itself had, in fact, been forgotten. Meanwhile, in Greece, time, decline, political conquest and the Orthodox Church had all worked towards consigning pagan Hellas to oblivion. Already in the late classical period Constantinople had replaced Athens as the centre of the Greek world, and the inhabitants of the Greek peninsula, if they were remembered at all, were regarded only as subjects of the Eastern Christian province of the Roman Empire. In the Byzantine world a 'Hellene' meant a pagan, and the name Hellas was used to designate the military and administrative district of eastern and central Greece.

This is not to say, however, that a tradition of Hellenistic culture had not been maintained by the Byzantines. A revival of classical learning had occurred at the time of the Schism between the Eastern and Western branches of the Christian Church in the eleventh and thirteenth centuries, when Byzantine scholars began to reassess their position and to lay claim to a Hellenic inheritance distinct from the Graeco-Roman tradition. To the Byzantine philosophers Psellus, and later Gemistus-Pletho, the leaders of this Hellenizing movement,[2]

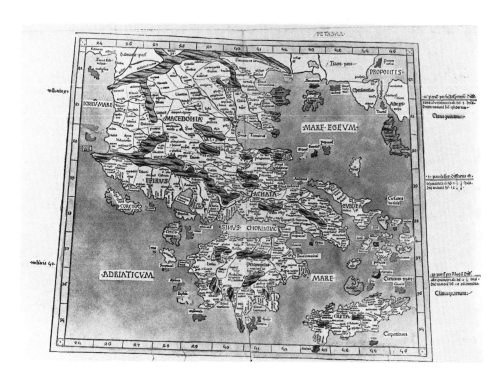

Map of Greece. From Ptolemy's *Geographia*, 1477

the inhabitants of the Greek peninsula were the direct descendants of the ancient Hellenes. In Europe at large, however, the impact of such ideas was limited: medieval historians did not even attribute a specific geographical location to Greece.

By the fourteenth century a considerable body of literature on contemporary Greece had been produced in Europe, much of it classical in origin, which, combined with a patchwork of travellers' tales and romances, created an idiosyncratic and fanciful image of Greece. Mandeville's description in his *Travels*, published in 1357, is characteristic:

> Abouten *Grece* there ben many Iles, as *Calistre, Calcas, Critige, Tesbria, Mynea, Flaxon, Melo, Carpate* and *Lempne* . . . And there ben many dyvers Langages and many Contreys, that ben obedyent to the Emperour; that is to seyn *Turcople, Pyneynard, Cornange,* and manye othere, as *Trachye,* and *Macedoigne,* of the whiche *Alisandre* was Kyng. In this Contree was *Aristotle* born, in a Cytee that Men clepen *Stragers,* a lytil fro the Cytee of *Trachye.* And at *Stragers* lythe *Aristotle;* and there is an Awtier upon his Toumbe: And there maken Men grete Festes of hym every zeer, as thoughe he were a Seynt. And at his Awtier thei holden here grete Conseilles and here Assembleez: And thei hopen, that thorghe inspiracioun of God and of him, thei schulle have the better Conseille. In this Contree . . . there is a gret Hille, that Men clepen *Olympus* . . . And it is so highe, that it passeth the Cloudes. And there is another Hille, that is clept *Athos,* that is so highe, that the Schadewe of hym rechethe to *Lempne,* that is an Ile . . .[3]

Already in the thirteenth century the Byzantine Empire had been dismembered and shared out amongst the leaders of the Fourth Crusade, who had conquered Constantinople in 1204. The Greek peninsula was then divided into numerous small Frankish states, while the Ionian Islands, the coast of the southern Peloponnesus and most of the Aegean Islands were taken by the Venetians. Untraversed by any of the major trade routes between West and

View of Chios. From G. Braun and
F. Hogenberg, *Civitates Orbis
Terrarum*, 1572–1618

East and possessing no major trade centres of its own, the Greek mainland
remained, for the most part, isolated and unknown except for the southern
coast of the mainland and the islands of the archipelago which had been
familiar to Europeans from an early period as a result of their trading
connections and the pilgrimages to the Holy Land. Indeed, a map of Greece is
included in the earliest edition of Ptolemy's *Geographia*, published at Bologna in
1477, and the important islands of the archipelago feature separately in all the
medieval *isolario* and *portolano* charts. Cristoforo Buondelmonti's *Isolario*, for
example, dated 1420, was exclusively concerned with the Greek islands.[4] By
the sixteenth century Crete, Rhodes and Chios had all developed into important
commercial centres. A view of Chios in Braun and Hogenberg's *Civitates Orbis
Terrarum* (1572-1618) shows a well-built town with a busy port. Of Chios,
Nicolas de Nicolay wrote in his *Navigations* (1567):

The island is divided into two parts . . . the upper is coarse and mountainous with
many forests and shady valleys and many rivulets which run down to the sea and
move the windmills to motion . . . The port is very good and capable of taking many
ships, and the city surrounded by good walls, large ramparts and deep waters. At one
of the corners of the public square . . . is the arcade where the merchants gather daily,
as they do in the Exchange at Lyons and Anvers to sell their merchandise. The streets
are large and beautiful . . . the houses and churches are built like those of Italy.[5]

In the early fifteenth century interest in Hellenic studies, along with the
influence of the Byzantine scholar Gemistus-Pletho and his pupils Manuel
Chrysoloras and Ioannes Argyropoulos, broadened European cultural
perspectives.[6] The enthusiasm of European humanists for the recovery of
classical Greek literature was also fostered by the Byzantine émigré scholars
who fled to the West after the fall of Constantinople to the Turks in 1453.[7]

Before the end of the fifteenth century the works of most of the ancient Greek historians, poets and philosophers, from Homer to Plotinus, were available in Latin translations. But the rediscovery of Greek philosophy and literature that stirred fifteenth-century Europe did not draw its inspiration directly from Greece but from the Graeco-Roman and Hellenistic traditions. It is not surprising, therefore, that while Europeans avidly studied Greek manuscripts, admired and collected Greek coins and expressed their fascination for Roman copies of lost Greek sculptures, they showed little interest in Greece itself and in its contemporary inhabitants. In Hartmann Schedel's *Liber Chronicarum* of 1492, for instance, Athens is depicted as a characterless Northern European-looking town; and in most European maps, such as Sebastian Munster's map of Greece in his *Cosmographia* (1555), Athens is indicated as 'Setines'. It was left to the German Hellenist Martinus Crusius to publish in 1584 accounts that he had collected from Greek scholars of the city of Athens as it actually was.[8] 'The most famous and free of all cities is now enslaved and even its glorious name has perished,' he was told by the Greek scholar Franciscus Portus. And the Italian traveller Ciriaco d'Ancona was exceptional in studying the ancient temples during his visits to Greece in the first half of the fifteenth century.[9]

Although interest in Greece was continually growing, throughout the sixteenth century the European image of Greece was still shaped by the experiences of pilgrims to the Holy Land and by the impressions of Levant merchants. On an ecclesiastical level, the attitude of the Roman Catholic peoples of Western Europe to the Orthodox Christian was not altogether favourable. Certainly, prints of Greek priests and monks, and accounts of the religious habits of the Greeks, featured in almost every illustrated travel-book of the sixteenth and seventeenth centuries, but there was a broad strand of denigration, despite continual attempts to heal the rift between the Catholic West and the Orthodox East. Warnings abound against the Orthodox Church, and Greeks are called 'sinners' and 'heretics' and portrayed as dominated by a hypocritical clergy. This contempt for Orthodoxy is borne out by the illustrations in André Thevet's *Cosmographie de Levant* (1554), while a century

An Orthodox Priest. From André Thevet, *Cosmographie de Levant,* 1554

View of Setines (Athens). From Hartmann Schedel, *Liber Chronicarum,* 1493

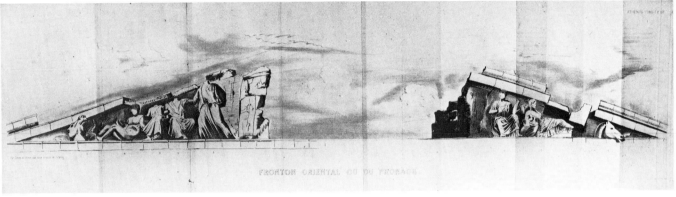

later his compatriot Sieur de la Croix, Secretary to the French Embassy at Constantinople, could write:

Jacques Carrey, *The West and East Pediments of the Parthenon*, 1674

> The Greeks do not believe that the Holy Ghost proceeds also from the Son. Therefore, the Holy Ghost which is a granter of light has ceased to illuminate them. As long as the Church recognized the Pope as its leader, it was flourishing, pure and brilliant. But since it abandoned Catholicism, and its sons have despised its Leader, it fell to misery, despised and disgraced because it had lost its splendour and grandeur. God's hand fell heavily upon the Greek Church and the thunder of Holy Wrath hurled down the Greeks from their proud glory to the abyss of ignorance and slavery.[10]

What increasingly focused attention on Greece for its own sake was its antiquities and the hope of finding them: they were the magnet which drew greater and greater numbers of connoisseurs, artists and aristocratic travellers to Greece. The earliest European collections of antiquities all date from the early seventeenth century when royal emissaries were employed by the English and French courts. Among such emissaries were Sir Kenelm Digby, who delighted Charles I with a series of 'old Greek marble-bases, columns and altars' which he brought back from a diplomatic mission to the Mediterranean in 1628, and Sir Thomas Roe, the English ambassador to Constantinople from 1621 to 1628, who acted as agent for two of the greatest English collectors, the Duke of Buckingham and the Earl of Arundel. The latter, as Henry Peacham remarked in his *Complete Gentleman* (1634), intended to 'transplant old Greece into England'. Louis XIV organized special missions, such as that headed by Colbert's protégé, the Marquis de Nointel, who explored the Aegean Islands in 1673-4 with a team of scholars and artists,[11] among them Jacques Carrey, the first artist to make detailed drawings of the pediments of the Parthenon. Of

15

PIAZZA DI CALAMATA

Vicenzo Maria Coronelli, *The Siege of Kalamata by the Venetian Army,* 1685–6

great use to these travellers and antiquaries was the first detailed map of Athens which was produced by the French Capuchin monks, who had founded a monastery in Athens in 1667 next to the Demosthenes Lantern (as the Lysicrates Monument was then called).[12]

Growing interest in antiquity was not, however, divorced from political events. As traders, the Venetians were initially the champions of Christendom against the Turks. By the early sixteenth century the Venetian trade hegemony in the Levant was eclipsed by the French, English and Dutch who, each in turn, succeeded in extracting privileges from the Ottoman Porte. Crete, the last Venetian fortress within the Ottoman Empire, fell in 1669 after a siege of twenty years. And it was the siege of Crete that drew the attention of Europe to political and military events in the Levant, at the same time creating a market for the series of illustrated publications that appeared depicting the various stages of the Veneto-Turkish War. Moreover, important new geographical surveys were undertaken under Venetian auspices, such as the series by Coronelli. In addition, Venetian army engineers made careful plans and drawings of the main battlefields. Yet the effect of the war on Greek monuments was disastrous, and in 1687 the Parthenon was irreparably damaged by Venetian artillery. But the Venetian occupation of Attica and the Morea in 1685-7 did have the general effect of making Greece more accessible to European travellers. Thus, in 1685, the first book dedicated exclusively to a part of the Greek mainland appeared, *The Present State of the Morea*, by the Englishman Bernard Randolph.

The Bombardment of the Parthenon by the Venetian Army on 26 September 1687. After G. M. Verneda

View of Misithra (Mistras). From Bernard Randolph, *The Present State of the Morea,* 1685

This opening up of new areas of Greece reinforced the lure of antiquities and led to an increase in the number of European travellers visiting the country during the last quarter of the seventeenth century. Among them, in 1675-6, were the French doctor Jacob Spon and the English naturalist George Wheler who went to Athens, Pausanias under arm, taking detailed notes of all the ancient monuments they came across. The illustrations in Spon's book *Voyage d'Italie, de Dalmatie, de Grèce et du Levant* long remained the closest to an accurate representation of the Parthenon that Europe possessed. Spon and Wheler were, in fact, the first travellers to write about Greece in a way that combined scholarship with first-hand observation.

During the eighteenth century antiquarianism and the expansion of European trade continued to give impetus to European interest in the Mediterranean. One factor which was of the utmost importance to the Greek cause was the virtual collapse of the Ottoman Empire as a unitary state and the emergent autonomy of its regions. At the same time, a shift in the European balance of power occurred: Venice was no longer a great power, and Russia came forward as the champion of the Greeks. As an Orthodox, rather than a Roman Catholic power, Russia had a specific affinity with Greece. Under Catherine the Great (1762-92), Russia made systematic attempts to subvert the authority of the Ottoman Empire in Greece by means of the Orthodox Church. In the first years of the Russo-Turkish War of 1770–4 Russian agents were active in Greece and encouraged the rising of the Morea.[13]

Direct experience of Greek art became possible in the eighteenth century largely through the archaeological excavations at Herculaneum and Pompeii and

Jacob Spon, *The Tower of the Winds*. From *Voyage d'Italie, de Dalmatie, de Grèce et du Levant*, 1678

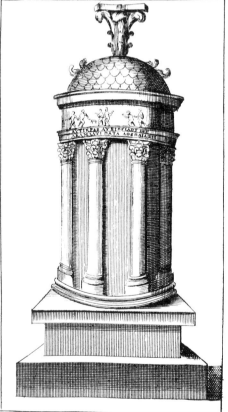

Jacob Spon, *The Lysicrates Monument*. From *Voyage d'Italie, de Dalmatie, de Grèce et du Levant*, 1678

the discovery of the Greek temples at Paestum. The English Society of Dilettanti – a club of aristocratic connoisseurs whose aim was to promote the 'Grecian taste' – and the German classicist Johann Joachim Winckelmann were the protagonists in this process of recognition and advancement of the Greek style. In 1751 James Stuart and Nicholas Revett were sent to Athens by the Society of Dilettanti in order to survey and make systematic measurements of the classical monuments. In 1758 the French architect Julien David Le Roy published his *Ruines des plus beaux monuments de la Grèce*, with grossly inaccurate depictions of classical monuments in fanciful Rococo settings. Indeed, exactness of illustration was not Le Roy's aim. As he wrote in the preface to the second edition of his book:

Julien David Le Roy, *An Imaginary Greek Landscape*, 1759

When publishing . . . the Ruins of ancient edifices . . . one could aim . . . at presenting servilely the measurements; and the most scrupulous exactness, when measuring them, constitutes, according to Mr Stuart, almost the only merit that a book of this kind may possess. I confess that I have very different views on the subject. And surely, I would not have travelled to Greece simply to observe the relation of the edifices and their parts with the divisions of our feet . . . These ruins, in the views which I have presented, occupy a much greater part of the picture than those of Mr Stuart; they thus affect the spectator more vividly, and succeed in passing on to his soul all the admiration by which one is stricken when looking at the Monuments themselves.

But when the first volume of Stuart and Revett's *Antiquities of Athens* appeared four years later, it was immediately recognized as being unquestionably superior to any other work, although full depictions of Doric architecture were not to be seen until the third volume was published in 1794.

If this magnificent publication sponsored by the Society of Dilettanti preserved what remained of ancient Greek architecture in depictions that were both accurate and beautiful, the spirit of ancient Hellas was most vividly evoked by Johann Joachim Winckelmann. 'Good taste was born under the sky of Greece,' he wrote in his *Gedanken über die Nachahmung der griechischen Werke in der Malerei und Bildhauerkunst* (Reflections on the Imitation of Greek Works in Painting and Sculpture), published in 1755. In his *Geschichte der Kunst des Alterthums* (History of the Art of Antiquity), published in 1764, Winckelmann proclaimed the 'superior humanity of the Greeks' and revealed to the European public a glowing picture of the conditions which had fostered creative activity in ancient Greece. The process of idealization of the classical golden age had begun. Winckelmann's view that the supreme ideals of human life and culture had been embodied in classical Greece came to be widely shared throughout Europe.

One of the effects of promoting these ideals was an increased demand for information about Greece. As a result, many European authors started writing about the life and sensibility of the ancient Greeks. In her *Letters* (1763), which were much praised by Voltaire, Lady Mary Wortley Montagu described, for instance, her impressions from a tour of the Greek islands:

'Tis impossible to imagine anything more agreeable than this journey could have been between 2 and 3,000 years since, when, after drinking a dish of tea with Sappho, I might have gone the same evening to visit the Temple of Homer in Chios, and have passed this voyage in taking plans of magnificent temples, delineating the miracles of statuaries, and conversing with the most polite and most gay of human kind![14]

C. A. Demoustier's *Lettres à Emilie sur la mythologie* (1786), consisting mainly of sentimental dissertations and poems on the deeds of the heroes of Greek mythology, was a book which proved very popular at the turn of the century. Johann J. W. Heinse's novel *Ardinghello und die glückseligen Inseln* (Ardinghello and the Happy Islands), published in 1787, presented a view of a society modelled according to Platonic ideals, while in the Abbé Barthélemy's popular *Voyage du jeune Anacharsis en Grèce*, published in 1788, a young Scythian tours Greece, seeking happiness from an enlightened nation. The description of Anacharsis' voyage revealed the most idyllic panorama of the ancient world. The book went through forty editions and was translated into all the main European languages. Finally, the adventures of a young Englishman in Greece are described in *Der Zauberer Angelion in Elis* (The Magician Angelion in Elis) by C. F. Benkowitz, published in 1798.

In the imaginary realm that was the European vision of Greece in the eighteenth century, ancient Greek life was pure, simple, and moral. Classical Hellas was, after Winckelmann, the source to which artists had to look for the ideals of 'noble simplicity and grandeur'. *Le goût grec* was reflected in a whole range of artistic activities, in art and in literature, in furniture and the decorative arts, in costume, even in coiffure. Graecomania knew no bounds: the Greek style became a way of life. But although perfection is possible in the imagination, soon Europe could no longer avert her eyes from events that would cloud this image, an image which was based largely on memories of the past.

The emergence of modern Greece

THE PROPAGATION of classical ideas continued in the nineteenth century, but the moralistic connotations embodied in the eighteenth-century rehabilitation of the ancient Greek world were gradually to be replaced by an appreciation of its aesthetic qualities only. Deprived of high-minded ideals, the return to an idea of 'beauty' embodied in Hellas became an end in itself. Greek became synonymous with the stylistically fashionable. Classical associations in art and literature became more explicit and formalized, while classical forms and ideas about art were popularized in order to make them accessible to as large a public as possible. Examples of this were Julius von Voss's comedy *Die Griechheit* (Greekness) first performed in 1807, which told the story of a baron who transformed his village into a Hellenic state; and August von Kotzebue's play *Die Ruinen von Athen* (The Ruins of Athens), which was performed in 1812 at the Royal Theatre of Budapest with music by Beethoven. An article in the French newspaper *Le Globe*, in 1820, epitomized the changing attitude towards Greece: 'We should not judge the Greeks from the way they are presented to us in the tragedies. These antique characters may express noble feelings and elevated passions, but . . . they are in fact people like us who feel all the emotions of humanity and reveal them in a language that it is possible for everyone to understand.'[1]

In Napoleonic Europe the pure forms of Greek art were gradually abandoned in favour of a florid Roman decorativeness, but at the same time Greek art and architecture were being discovered afresh by English architects. A wide interest in ancient Greece was late to develop fully in England. In the architectural world it was not until after the publication of the third volume of Stuart and Revett's *Antiquities of Athens* in 1794, with depictions of monuments of the Doric order, and the rejection by Thomas Hope of James Wyatt's Roman designs for Downing College, Cambridge, in 1804, that the Greek style became established in England.[2] English classical scholars were stirred into activity: 'Those who come after me shall have nothing to glean. Not only every temple, but every stone and every inscription shall be copied with the most scrupulous fidelity,' wrote the twenty-six-year-old Cambridge scholar John Tweddell when he set out to visit Greece early in 1799.[3] In the spring of that year he was in Athens, in company with the French artist François Préaux, his draughtsman. Tweddell's zeal was the cause of his death a few months later, and he joined the select list of European travellers to be buried in the Theseum – 'that English mausoleum' as the Reverend Thomas Smart Hughes called it – with a fragment of the Parthenon as his tombstone.

A visit to Greece and the careful study of its surviving monuments came to be regarded as an essential part of the professional training of a Greek Revival architect. William Wilkins, a leader of the Greek Revival in England, visited Greece in 1801, and he was followed two years later by Robert Smirke. Smirke and his companion, the painter William Walker, toured Attica and the Morea. 'How can I, by description, give you any idea of the great pleasure I enjoyed in the sight of these ancient buildings,' Smirke wrote to his father; 'those in Rome (with a few exceptions) soon grow in some degree uninteresting but have now sunk into disregard and contempt in my mind.'[4] Before the end of the second decade of the nineteenth century most of the remains of the classical Greek

Johann Karl Haller von Hallerstein, *View of the Theseum*, 1810

orders had been studied *in situ* by Charles Robert Cockerell, Charles Barry, William Kinnaird, John Foster, George Ledwell Taylor, Edward Cresy, John Sanders, Thomas Allason and Francis Arundale. All were eager to reveal new aspects of the known monuments, and some were lucky enough to discover new architectural treasures hidden in the Greek lands. Thus, Allason was the first to observe the *entasis* of the Greek columns, while G. L. Taylor chanced to trip over the Lion of Chaeronea, as he describes in his Greek journal:

When approaching the place my horse made a fearful stumble over a stone nearly buried in the road, and on looking back, I was struck with the faint appearance of sculpture on the stone . . . Calling a halt, we all turned back, and having satisfied ourselves, by removing the earth with our riding whips, that it was sculpture, we engaged some peasants . . . and did not leave the spot until we had dug up the colossal head of the lion, and some of his limbs separated.[5]

Others combined professional expertise with a greater appetite for treasure-hunting. The most spectacular group with such motives was the international archaeological expedition that excavated the temples at Aegina and Bassae.[6] In 1811 the architects C. R. Cockerell and John Foster, the German Baron Haller von Hallerstein and the Swabian painter Jacob Linckh discovered the greater part of the sculptures from the Temple of Aphaea in Aegina. The following year the team was joined by the Livonian painter Baron Otto Magnus von Stackelberg, the Danish archaeologist Peter Olaf Brönsted and Georg Christian

Gropius, who later became the Austrian consul at Athens. This time they excavated at Bassae, where they discovered the frieze of the Temple of Apollo Epicurius. The group formed a society named Xenion, the essential membership qualification of which was 'enthusiasm for Greece, ancient literature and the Fine Arts', and swore an oath of mutual assistance. When their archaeological endeavours ended, they took the greatest care to secure the export of their priceless discoveries.[7] The frieze from Bassae was finally bought by the British Museum, while the sculptures from Aegina were bought by Crown Prince Ludwig of Bavaria and exhibited at the Munich Pinakothek.

As in previous centuries, the lure of antiquity, or of antiques to be collected, was the magnet that drew European travellers to Greece. The Scottish artist Hugh William Williams wrote in his *Travels*:

For centuries past there has been a trade in the antiquities of Greece, both in medals and sculpture. Whatever relics could be picked up, readily found purchasers among the strangers and merchants who visit this interesting country; consequently, they are spread over a great part of Europe, and there is hardly a collection of any note, which cannot boast of some specimens of Grecian art. When all this is considered, it appears surprising that any valuable remains should still be found, in a country where so little pains is taken to make discoveries by excavation. Grecian marbles and coins may be purchased at Rome, Paris, London, or even Petersburg, at as cheap a rate as in this country.[8]

Indeed, architectural and archaeological research in Greece led unavoidably to official and unofficial excavations and consequently to the export of antiquities.

Charles Robert Cockerell, *Excavations at the Temple of Aphaea in Aegina*, 1811

The most spectacular instance of this was the Earl of Elgin's purchase of the Parthenon frieze. In September 1799 Elgin had been sent as the English ambassador to the Ottoman Porte, and he immediately started making preparations for his plan to make his embassy 'beneficial to the progress of the Fine Arts in Great Britain'.[9] In August 1800 Elgin's agent, the Italian landscape draughtsman Lusieri, was in Athens as the head of an expedition that included the 'painter of Figures', Theodor (or Feodor) Iwanovitch from Central Asia – nicknamed 'Elgin's Calmuck' – and two Italian architects, Vicenzo Balestra and Sebastiano Ittar. Elgin's success in acquiring permission for his artists to work on the Acropolis was due to the particular political situation in the Mediterranean. Bonaparte's conquest of Egypt had had a great effect on the relations between France and Turkey. The Battle of the Nile, and the subsequent Turkish declaration of war on France, gave the British government an opportunity to supersede France in the favour of the Ottoman Porte. It was after the successful British expedition to Egypt that Elgin had been awarded the *firman* by the sultan.[10]

Most travellers were eager collectors whenever they had the chance, even those who condemned Elgin's activities. The classical scholar Edward Daniel Clarke, for instance, left moving eye-witness accounts of Lusieri's depredations on the Acropolis.[11] Nonetheless, he himself was able to build up a collection of coins and manuscripts during his Greek tour in 1801-2, and also to secure the colossal statue of Ceres from Eleusis, today in the Fitzwilliam Museum, Cambridge.

But collections of antiquities were not only to be found outside Greece. The Reverend Thomas Smart Hughes, who firmly 'resisted every instigation to follow the example of many travellers in commencing excavations',[12] was greatly impressed by Lusieri's collection in Athens; Herr Gropius, the Austrian

Benjamin Robert Haydon, *Torso of Dionysus Exhibited in the Park Lane Museum*, 1809

Charles Robert Cockerell, *Lord Elgin's Museum at Park Lane*, 1808

p.2

consul at Athens, was also a collector. Despite the fact that the numerical superiority of British traveller-collectors caused all foreigners to be addressed as 'Mylordi' by the Greeks,[13] the antiquities market in Attica at the beginning of the early nineteenth century was largely monopolized by a Frenchman, the artist Louis François Sébastien Fauvel, who held the post of French consul at Athens from 1803.[14] Fauvel was the cicerone of every learned traveller in Athens and its neighbourhood. An eager and skilful excavator, he transformed his house into a rich and well-organized museum. There were sculptures, vases, inscriptions, plaster casts from the sculptures of the Temple of Aphaea, even detailed maps of Athens prepared on the basis of his own excavations. Another Frenchman whose name was connected with the antiques market was the Comte de Marcellus. An attaché at the French Embassy at Constantinople, Marcellus negotiated in 1820 the purchase of a female statue that had recently been discovered on the island of Melos by Colonel Voutier.[15] The Venus de Milo was thus added to the trophies of the European antiquarians.

It would be unfair to state that the interest of Europeans in Greece was entirely motivated by materialistic considerations. In the first decade of the nineteenth century European researches in Greece were stimulated by an interest in topographical studies. The then current European fascination with the identification of 'Homeric sites'[16] was only one aspect of a new concern for the authentication of classical antiquity. But if Troy provided an interesting field for topographical investigation, Greece was an altogether more exciting prospect. Vital resources of information were available in Greek lands which could not only amplify the literary material, but would also serve to check it. Sir William Gell, Byron's 'Coxcomb Gell', was in Greece in 1804; two years later, in company with Edward Dodwell, he explored Ithaca for the light it might be expected to throw on its ancient history and the veracity of the Homeric descriptions. Gell's *Itinerary in Greece* (1819) was a popular pocket-guide for travellers in the mainland. Dodwell, Gell's companion, an antiquarian, classical scholar and collector, had already visited Greece in 1801. His *Classical and Topographical Tour through Greece* (1819) is at once a systematic topographical description and a detailed investigation into the remains of antiquity.

In the early nineteenth century Greece had become a fashionable meeting-place for tourists of all nationalities. John Cam Hobhouse, Byron's travel-companion to Greece, wrote in his *Journey through Albania* (1813):

At the period when every young man of fortune, in France and England, considered it an indispensable part of his education to survey the monuments of ancient art remaining in Italy, only a few desperate scholars and artists ventured to trust themselves amongst the barbarians, to contemplate the ruins of Greece. But these terrors, which a person who has been on the spot cannot conceive could ever have been well-founded, seem at last to be dispelled; Attica at present swarms with travellers . . . and . . . a few more years may furnish the Piraeus with all the accommodations of a fashionable watering-place.[17]

The Comte de Forbin was annoyed by the invasion of European artists in Athens in 1819:

I met there many artists, English or German, drawing, measuring, endlessly and with the minute exactness of the most scrupulous commentator, those monuments, those noble creations of genius. Miserable slaves of rules, of the lightest caprice of the ancients, they write whole volumes in order to correct a mistake . . . concerning the measurements of an architrave. They establish themselves in Athens for eight years in order to draw three columns . . . and it is only after the efforts of many years that their sad watercolours reach the highest degree of boring perfection.[18]

As well as recording the classical monuments, however, European artists were also interested in depicting the scenery within and around the ruins. Yet their depictions of the Greek landscape seem to have been largely tinted as a result of an intellectual process – characteristically, written descriptions often seen to have been more accurate than pictorial representations. To a European traveller, to visit Greece in the early nineteenth century was to visit an ideal.

It is to this ancient theatre of the arts that we call the artists of our country. Painters, sculptors, it is in the plains of Arcadia, by the banks of Eurotas . . . that you will collect a harvest of new and sublime ideas. There you will discover the Greek form in all its primitive beauty . . . You will not deny that the ancient ideal can only be found in the scenery there, which is so perfect that it surpasses the imagination . . . Landscape painters, come to this land: the sun shines here in all its splendour in an azure sky, free from those grey mists that so often obscure it in your climates, and give to objects a uniform tint. How many memories will spring to mind when studying this landscape! Here a column, standing amidst the ruins, will help you retrace the outlines of a temple

Antoine Laurent Castellan, *A Greek Shepherd*, 1808

. . . further down a savage grotto . . . will remind you of a golden age. The landscape painter may also glance in the middle of a fertile plain, the labourer guiding his simple plough pulled by two oxen. And so in his turn he will be able to cry *Et in Arcadia ego* and compose pictures worthy of Poussin.

Thus claimed the French painter A.L. Castellan during a tour of the Peloponnesus.[19] Indeed, the influences of tradition, history and literature were such that the pleasure of a visit to Athens, Delphi, Marathon or Sparta must ultimately have been more intellectual than visual. Moreover, it was generally thought that the visitor's physical presence at an actual site would stimulate almost miraculously a revival of its ancient ethos. The concept of the 'spirit of place' which Greece seemed to offer was attractive, to say the least, and Europeans were eager to experience it: 'It is for the sake of Greece that I abandoned my friends and relatives,' writes the Italian Saverio Scrofani in his *Viaggio* (1799); and he explains: 'One might ask: could I not, perhaps, read other travellers' accounts in order to find out all that I want to know about Greece? No, I did not want to make the journey in order to learn, but in order to feel.' European artists and their clients shared the belief that certain places which had been dignified by past glory possessed such powers of suggestion that their successful depiction could stimulate the imagination and make more vivid the impression of what had happened there. For example, Karl Rottmann's *Lake Copais* shows a deserted site, but with his impressive   Pl. XIV* treatment of light and the firm construction of the landscape the artist achieves an alluring emotional effect. The painting aims successfully at effects of solemnity and stillness, evocative of an ancient world of timeless truth. In the *View of Olympia*, by the same artist, the serenity of the composition makes the   Pl. XXIV scene very appealing to the literary imagination. Yet to harmonize classical literature and painting was not an easy task. In many cases the artists tried to give monumental expression by unnecessarily dramatic compositions, as did W. H. Bartlett, for example, in his *Temple of Minerva at Sunium*.   Pl. 54

*For plates I–XXX see colour sections; for plates 1–78 see pp. 82–175

If such a procedure showed a lack of fidelity to the actual appearance of the Greek landscape, it also came to reveal, surprisingly, an ignorance of the intended, intimate association between classical Greek sites and their setting. In Greece, local features were a determining influence in the creation of mythological associations within a particular setting and these sites would then become sacred. It is this intimate association between myth, history and geography that is one of the distinguishing elements of Greek landscape. Indeed, as has been emphasized in recent literature,[20] it is possible to trace the basis of Greek mythology to the action and reaction of landscape and imagination: many myths may be seen as revealing the origins of natural phenomena or as explaining peculiarities in nature. The skill with which the ancients appropriated to their different deities the abodes best suited to their temper and character was of a very high order. What strikes the visitor to the ancient *temena* (sites of pilgrimage) even today is not only the creation of magnificent architectural ensembles, but also the way in which such sites have been chosen, that is, the way in which the devotional aspect ascribed to them is matched by and revealed in their natural placement and configuration. At Delphi, for example, the site of the Sanctuary of Apollo, surrounded by massively carved rocks and commanding dramatic views across the plain, was peculiarly calculated to the sublimity which the presence of the god excited. Similarly, the Temple of Bassae, designed by the architect of the Parthenon, seems to have been deliberately situated on the edge of an impressive plateau to take advantage of the sublime effect which the remote and wild site evokes.

In the first decades of the nineteenth century, none of the ancient sites had been excavated and the few remains that were to be seen could hardly compare with the descriptions of towns and sanctuaries given by the ancient writers. Nevertheless, their natural surroundings were still revealing. For although the classical rivers had diminished in volume and idyllic woods had dwindled in extent, the general features of the landscape remained. Surprisingly, however, the relationship between ruins and their natural environment was in fact quite different from that which most European artists suggest in their views. The majority of such views are, in terms of hard information, of little use for providing a picture of Greece in the nineteenth century. In their search for mood and effect, the artists were frequently uninterested in investigating the actual features of the landscape they drew. Sketching under the discomfort of a scorching sun, they later selected and re-arranged motifs, eliminating what they considered unnecessary. Moreover, the majority of artists, influenced by the conventions of the day, depicted the Greek scenery in a Claudian diffused light that tended to blur forms until they seemed part of the very iridescence of the atmosphere. But in Greece there are no mists, no half tones. Even in these days of industrial pollution, Greece is remarkable for the sharpness of the light, the transparent brightness of its sky. The atmosphere of Greece being so pure and luminous, the spectator could distinguish great distances 'even more than 300 miles', Edward Dodwell remarked, and details in the distance appeared clearer and therefore required an accuracy of delineation which is rare in nineteenth-century depictions.

What European artists and their clients really wanted, however, were images that revealed the scenery of the imagined classical Greek world, a world that was mythologized according to their expectations. Once again, it was the formalized, literary past, not the present, that was the attraction of Greece. 'There is nothing in our visit resembling the introduction to a new circle of acquaintances; it is the revived delight of the society of long absent and beloved friends,' wrote the artist and poet William Haygarth when he stepped onto Greek soil.[21] This illusion presented a challenge to the artist. Although similar in some ways to the problem of depicting the classical sites of Italy, it involved additional difficulties. In nineteenth-century Italy there still existed picturesque villages, magnificent buildings, a rich countryside; but in Greece, decline through long periods of wars and foreign domination had resulted in depopulation and the impoverishment of both people and landscape. When depicting Athens the artist could justifiably believe, as far as general features went, that – barring the Turkish mosques – he was looking at the same view of the Acropolis as Pericles and Socrates. But he would try in vain to recognize from the few scattered trees at Thermopylae the oak forest which was there and which is evoked so vividly by Herodotus. And in Thebes, another famous site, the temples had been swept away and the surrounding hills looked arid and bare.

Thus, most of the early nineteenth-century Greek views provide only a barely adequate representation of a temple or a well-known architectural group, framed by an appropriate yet vaguely defined landscape setting and enveloped in a pervading air of antiquity. The actual surroundings are replaced or modified according to the effect the artist wished to convey. The scenery was subordinated to the motif, which was, after all, the view's principal recommendation to its prospective buyers – for it was the legendary Greece rather than the contemporary reality that the public preferred. In this way, artists made an effort to satisfy the curiosity of those who had not travelled to Greece and to remind those who had of their experiences in the country. To either group, no object was more likely to awaken a train of reflections connected with what they had seen or read about Greece than the image of the Acropolis of Athens. It mattered little whether it was depicted through a mass of dense foliage, or surrounded by barren rocks. What was important was whether the picture matched the emotionally loaded impressions that the tourist associated with Athens. In the end, the identification titles of these landscape views came to lose their significance. It is hard even for the most knowledgeable observer to identify the Mycenaean citadel, for instance, when its surrounding rocks, renowned for their bareness and wildness, are shown as undulating idyllic knolls; or the Attic hills, which are famous for their clear outlines, when depicted as misty volcanic mountains in order to contribute a sense of sublimity to the 'Acropolis Rock' they encircle. Again and again, in these nineteenth-century depictions, what one actually sees are fairyland views bathed in a haze of golden light – a visual cliché evocative of a golden age.

Without denying the sincerity of what the artists felt, it seems that an established convention of composition facilitated the expression of a particular emotion. Indeed, Claude and Poussin provided a convenient formula for the pictorial combination of nature and classical remains: in Joseph Cartwright's *Town of Corfu* the composition is closed on one side by a clump of trees, while a   Pl. 1 series of diagonals direct the eye of the observer towards the mountainous foreground in which a shepherd goes about his business with Arcadian ease; a typically Claudian *repoussoir* tree introduces William Haygarth's *View of*

Pls 7, 5 — *Ioannina*; even in Edward Lear's *View of Parga* the main scene is solidly placed in the middle ground and is framed by two perfectly balanced trees.

'Mr Gell presents his compliments to Miss Hawkins and sends proof positive that *he is not so unwise as to neglect the opportunity of getting a view coloured à la Poussin*. The view is that of Athens from the sacred way to Eleusis,' noted William Gell on the reverse of a drawing. His attitude was also shared by the Scottish artist Hugh William Williams:

The scenery in Athens demands . . . our most careful study . . . When nature presents her endless effects of beauty and of grandeur, the judgement may hesitate . . . Unless we are familiar with what has been discovered by her favourite sons, she will not present those electrifying truths, which flash upon the mind in studying her not only as she is, but as seen through the medium of works of genius . . . The works of Niccolo Poussin, Domenichino and Sebastian Bourdon agree with the character of Athens, as viewed at no great distance from the ancient buildings. The simple dignity of form and colour, perceptibly in the works of these great men, enters into the spirit of its story, and calls forth corresponding sentiments. The distant views of Athens claim the style of Claude; his unbroken lines, that continuity and taking up of parts, sweetly tranferring them to each other, and conveying to the mind the sentiment of beauty, well expresses what Athens is in her robes of silvery gray. The colouring too, of Claude is just and accurate, as referable to Greece in her remote and lovely scenes.[22]

Williams's Greek views earned him the name of 'Grecian' Williams. Reviewing his exhibition, held in Edinburgh in 1822, William Hazlitt wrote:

Here [in the Calton Convening Room] another Greece grows on the walls . . . ancient temples rise . . . As works of art, these watercolour drawings deserve very high praise . . . We have at once an impressive and satisfactory idea of the country of which we have heard so much . . . Some splenetic travellers have pretended that Attica was dry, flat and barren. But it is not so in Mr Williams's authentic draughts . . . and we thank him for restoring to us our old and, as it appears, true illusion.[23]

The artist William Linton is even more categorical about Claude's appropriateness for the realization of Greek views: 'The atmosphere of Greece is more in accordance with his [Claude's] taste than the drier and harsher one of Italy . . . Indeed Claude is often seen in Greece, and very rarely in Italy [*sic*], though he never visited the former country.'[24]

Pl. XXVI
Pls 27, XXV — Williams's Greek landscapes, as well as those by the majority of his contemporaries, do not express melancholy regret for what was then the relic of a vanished civilization. His *Temple of Aphaea in Aegina*, like William Page's *View of the Acropolis* and *View of Corinth*, are not 'ruin pieces'. The figures are appropriately small and are integrated harmoniously with the landscape as decorative elements in an aesthetic schema; dressed in their brightly coloured costumes, they either sit nonchalantly with their backs to the spectator amongst architectural remains, or guard their flocks like Virgilian shepherds. Such pictures are generalized evocations rather than particular images: no contemporary references are appropriate in this dream world. European spectators were thus given an opportunity of escaping into a lost paradise, a happy land of classical perfection which was, nevertheless, geographically real and fairly easily accessible

Throughout the first two decades of the nineteenth century, the majority of European artists and travellers who wandered about Greece were largely unappreciative of anything that had happened there since the age of Pericles. They knew exactly what they expected to find, and they found it. The one thing that their depictions excluded was the actual inhabitants of the country. Indeed, many Western visitors had little sympathy for the descendants of the Hellenes. For if the wild mountaineers of Mani could claim to be the direct descendants of Leonidas' warriors, contemporary Athenians hardly matched the visitors' expectations of what the disciples of Pericles should be like. What is more, contemporary Greeks seemed to have retained some of the less gratifying qualities of their ancestors – they were, for instance, as argumentative and stubborn as Achilles, and as cunning as Odysseus. Yet, increasingly, it occurred to the growing number of European visitors to Greece to question the validity of their expectations that these people now should conform to classical notions of virtue. Had they not, after all, been deprived of their natural rights for over four centuries? Had not Rousseau demonstrated that mankind was prone to degeneration when enslaved? And how could Europeans remain indifferent to the fate of the Greeks since Western civilization was supposed to be based on the values of the ancient Hellenes?

William Gell, *A View of Athens 'à la Poussin'*, 1800

I Eugène Delacroix, *A Greek Warrior*, c. 1820

In common with many contemporary European artists, Delacroix was profoundly inspired by the drama of the Greek struggle for independence. In 1821, following the outbreak of the Greek Revolution, he planned a picture 'whose subject I shall take from the current war between the Greeks and the Turks'; during the same period he began a series of studies incorporating the picturesque costumes of the combatants – the Greek pallikars *and the Turkish janissaries. It was these studies, based on actual costumes brought back to France by Jean Robert Auguste and other collectors, which were to culminate in Delacroix's first masterpiece on a Greek theme,* The Massacre of Scio, *exhibited at the Salon of 1824.*

II James Stuart, *Stuart Sketching the Erechtheum*, 1751

Eighteenth-century interest in Greek art was epitomized by James 'Athenian' Stuart and his collaborator Nicholas Revett who stayed in Athens from 1751 to 1753 meticulously examining the monuments and making excavations. Stuart's painting of himself sketching the Erechtheum was subsequently re-engraved for Stuart and Revett's monumental publication The Antiquities of Athens, *with the following description by Revett:*

'A View of the west end of the Temple of Minerva Polias, and of the Pandrosium. The Turkish Gentleman smoking a long pipe, is the Disdár-Agá, he leans on the shoulder of his son-in-law, Ibrahim Agá, and is looking at our labourers, who are digging to discover the Base, and the steps of the Basement under the Caryatides. He was accustomed to visit us from time to time, to see that we did no mischief to the Building; but in reality, to see that we did not carry off any treasure; for he did not conceive, any other motive could have induced us, to examine so eagerly what was under ground in his Castle. The two Turks in the Pandrosium were placed there by him to watch our proceedings; and give him an account of our discoveries. The little girl leading a lamb, and attended by a negro slave, is the daughter of Ibrahim Agá. The lamb is fatted to be eaten at the feast of the Beiram, which was not far off at the time this view was taken.'

James Stuart and Nicholas Revett, *The Antiquities of Athens Measured and Delineated*, vol. II, 1787

III Louis François Cassas, *Hadrian's Aqueduct*, 1775

The subject of several eighteenth-century 'ruin' studies, Hadrian's Aqueduct was demolished in 1778 by order of the Turkish governor to provide building materials for the walls of Athens.

'I left the Stadium and followed the Ilissus upstream. Turning left, I arrived at Mount Anchesmus, whose summit dominates the Acropolis, the Museum Hill and the Areopagus. . . . At the foot of Mount Anchesmus is a monument in the Ionic order which records that the Emperor Hadrian built an aqueduct on this spot in order to supply the city of Athens with water. According to the inscription, the aqueduct was completed and dedicated by the Emperor Antoninus Pius, in the year of his third consulship . . .'

Julien David Le Roy, *Ruines des plus beaux monuments de la Grèce*, 1758

I

II

III

IV

V

VI

'Tis living Greece no more

VII

IV Charles Lock Eastlake, *Byron's 'Dream'*, 1829

Byron's influence on British art reveals a less violent and less dramatic interpretation than that seen in the works of Delacroix and other European artists. In Eastlake's picture, based on the following lines from Byron's poem The Dream, *the scene is set in one of the 'sunny isles' of Greece. The poet is seen in the foreground, reposing among ruins.*

> '. . . and in the last he lay
> Reposing from the noontide sultriness,
> Couch'd among fallen columns, in the shade
> Of ruin'd walls that had survived the names
> Of those who rear'd them; by his sleeping side
> Stood camels grazing, and some goodly steeds
> Were fastened near a fountain; and a man
> Clad in a flowing garb did watch the while,
> While many of his tribe slumber'd around:
> And they were canopied by the blue sky,
> So cloudless, clear, and purely beautiful. . .'

Byron, *The Dream*, 1816

V E. F. Green, *Landscape with a Greek Girl*, 1835

By the middle of the nineteenth century, Greek costumes and embroideries had become a popular theme with European artists. The Greek lady depicted here is wearing an authentic city costume of the period, although her tall fez belongs to a man's costume.

VI Christian Perlberg, *Fête by the Olympieum*, 1838

The numerous holidays and entertainments of the Athenians provided ideal material for the nineteenth-century artist in search of the picturesque. On the last Monday of the end of Lent carnival, a big open-air festival called 'Koulouma' was held near the Olympieum.

'. . . it was the last day of the carnival, and . . . there would be a large congregation of the Athenians outside the town, at the columns of the Temple of Jupiter, to regale themselves with the simple refections of olives and bread, and the small wine of the country, and to amuse themselves with national dances. . . . I found the assembly very merry over their frugal repast. They had formed rings and some of them were dancing in the Albanian style. The quick motion of the Albanian dances is very similar to that of the Scotch, and the dancers also make a noise similar to the highland fling.'

George Cochrane, *Wanderings in Greece*, 1837

VII Joseph Mallord William Turner, *'T'is living Greece no more'*, 1822

The scene is Turner's earliest depiction of a 'Byronic' Greek subject and reveals the artist's use of Greece as a symbol of the ravages of time. The title is taken from Byron's poem The Giaour.

'Such is the aspect of this shore;
'Tis Greece, but living Greece no more! . . .
Shrine of the mighty! can it be,
That this is all remains of thee?'

Byron, *The Giaour*, 1813

Already by the end of the eighteenth century political and social developments in the Ottoman Empire had the effect of gradually awakening Europe to the existence of a contemporary Greece. The war of 1787-92 between Russia and Turkey had created the conditions for a series of spectacular developments which were favourable to the Greeks. In July 1770 the *Gentleman's Magazine* had commented: 'Half a century ago, no one would have believed that these savages would have risen to such heights . . . and who knows, but that the same people, may contend with the other maritime powers for the empire of the sea!' There was to be some truth in this. The Kuchuk Kainarji Agreement, which the Russians imposed on the Sultan in 1774, was very helpful to Greek merchants in that it enabled them to engage in trade without fear of taxation by the Porte. Greek merchants were thus able to extend their operations beyond Italy to France, Germany, Austria, Hungary and Russia. The extension in trade led to the growth of the Greek diaspora communities in the major trading centres of Western Europe: Vienna, Marseilles, Trieste, Odessa, Budapest and elsewhere. And this was, in turn, accompanied by an increase in intellectual activity prompted by the new, large, mercantile class, both inside and outside Greece.[25] The awareness of these thriving Greek communities made Europeans reconsider the received ideas they held of contemporary Greeks, and they began to wonder if the inhabitants of the Hellenic lands could be considered any longer as degenerate descendants of glorious ancestors.

Thus, in the travel literature of the period, parallels were often drawn between contemporary customs and those of the ancient Greeks, and some writers began to speculate on the future of the enslaved Greeks. The French scholar Pierre Augustin Guys, for example, declared in the preface to his *Voyage littéraire de la Grèce* (1771):

It is impossible to study ancient history without starting from the Greeks . . . Moreover, it is the traveller's duty, I believe, to examine whether the people who live in a country rich in so many ancient monuments are worthy of our attention . . . The fact that the Greeks have kept their character intact, is due to their deep faith that their customs and traditions are the only fortune that is left to them.[26]

J. L. David, *A Greek Funeral*. From Pierre Augustin Guys, *Voyage littéraire de la Grèce*, 2nd edition, 1776

Greece Expiring among Classical Ruins. From the Comte de Choiseul-Gouffier, *Voyage pittoresque de la Grèce*, vol. I, 1782

The illustrations in Guys's book, based on drawings by David, are contemporary in subject-matter, yet stylistically they still echo classical compositions. J. C. F. Hölderlin's *Hyperion oder der Eremit in Griechenland* (Hyperion or the Hermit in Greece) (1797–9) was a dithyrambic encomium of ancient Greece and, at the same time, an eloquent plea for a Greek political revival. The Comte de Choiseul-Gouffier's three-volume publication, *Voyage pittoresque de la Grèce* (1782–1812), abounds in views of the flourishing ports of the Aegean Islands. Moreover, the frontispiece to the first volume presented a precociously Philhellenic statement: Greece is depicted in chains, seated among the ruined tombs of Pericles, Themistocles and other Greek heroes, and behind her is inscribed in Latin 'Exoriare aliquis' (That an avenger might spring out of our bones).[27] 'Let it be said clearly', Choiseul-Gouffier writes in the introduction, 'there still exist in this country men ready to revive the memories of their ancestors.'

In the nineteenth century new themes began to surface in the travel literature on Greece. The Italian artist Simone Pomardi, for instance, who sold a large number of Greek sketches to Dodwell, was interested in everyday life. His *Viaggio della Grecia* (1820) abounds in descriptions of Greek customs. The same interest is manifested in the *Voyage à Smyrne, dans l'archipel et l'île de Candie* (1817) by the French diplomat J. M. Tancoigne. Count Etienne Szechenyi, a Hungarian who was one of the few Central European politicians to visit Greece, wrote enthusiastic accounts of the Greek schools he saw in Ioannina and Chios. But the most memorable publication of these years was *An Essay on Certain Points of Resemblance between the Ancient and Modern Greeks* (1813) by Frederick S. Douglas, the cousin of the renowned Earl of Guildford.

On another front, as the exploration of Greece coincided with the development of studies of natural history, European scientists became interested in recording the uniquely rich variety of Greek flora. The Bohemian botanist Franz Sieber collected specimens of Greek plants in the islands, while the standard work on Greek flora is still the beautifully illustrated series entitled *Flora Graeca* (1806-28), which was based on the researches of John Sibthorp at the turn of the nineteenth century.

p. 45

A Klepht. From François Charles Pouqueville, *Voyage dans la Grèce,* 2nd edition, 1826–7

There were also politically motivated surveys which were compiled by official representatives of foreign governments. Owing to the rivalry of European powers over the remains of the Ottoman Empire, Greece had been swarming with military and diplomatic missions since the beginning of the nineteenth century. In 1800 André Grasset-Saint-Sauveur, a commissioner of commercial relations of Napoleon, presented a thorough account of the Greek territories that had been acquired by the French in his three-volume *Voyage historique, littéraire et pittoresque dans les isles et possessions ci-devant vénitiennes du Levant.* The same year Félix de Beaujour, the French consul at Thessaloniki, published his *Tableau du commerce de la Grèce,* which is still a valuable source of information on the Greek economy at the turn of the century. In the early 1800s the indefatigable Colonel William Martin Leake carried out a most detailed survey of Greece for the British government.[28] The five-volume *Voyage dans la Grèce* (1825) by François Charles H. L. Pouqueville, Napoleon's consul at Ioannina, was also much praised for its comprehensiveness.

Certainly European visitors were not unanimous in their opinions of the Greeks. Indeed, some travellers could only be described as 'Mishellenes', while others figure later as members of one or other of the European committees for the Greek cause. In 1805, for instance, the Prussian scholar Jacob Salomon Bartholdy presented an image of the Greeks as 'a pile of dried trunks that alone testifies to what used to be a proud and noble forest' in his *Bruchstücke zur nähern Kenntniss des heutigen Griechenlands* (Fragments towards a Better Understanding of Present-day Greece). By contrast, the eventual outcome of the visit of the distinguished French printer Ambroise Firmin-Didot to Greece in 1816 was one of his greatest undertakings: the publication of his 'Bibliothèque des auteurs grecs' under the supervision of Adamantios Korais. In Chateaubriand's *Itinéraire de Paris à Jérusalem* (1811) the emotional narrative of the writer's short sojourn in Greece powerfully evokes the pathetic decadence of the country:

This picture of Attica, this spectacle which I contemplated, had been surveyed by eyes that have been shut to it for more than two thousand years . . . From the spot where we were placed, we might, in the prosperous times of Athens, have seen her fleets starting out from the Piraeus to engage the enemy, or to repair to the feasts of Delos; we might have heard the grief of Oedipus, of Philoctetes and of Hecuba bursting from the theatre of Bacchus; we might have heard the applause of the citizens, and the orations of Demosthenes. But alas! no sound met our ears, save a few shouts from an enslaved populace issuing at intervals from those walls which so long ago echoed to the voices of a free people.[29]

The European conscience came to feel ill at ease when confronted with such realities, and this feeling could only be heightened by Childe Harold's arrival on the scene in Byron's *Childe Harold's Pilgrimage* when it was published in 1812. Byron forced the condition of modern Greece on the imagination and conscience of Europe: Greece was no longer just the deserted abode of nymphs or muses. In Byron's obsession it was revealed as a passionate and colourful world that was still alive:

> *And yet how lovely in thine age of woe,*
> *Lands of lost Gods and godlike men! art thou!*
> *Thy vales of evergreen, thy hills of snow,*
> *Proclaim thee Nature's varied favourite now . . .*[30]

Ferdinand Bauer, *Vignette with a View of Parnassus.* From *Flora Graeca,* vol. I, 1806

FLORA

GRÆCA

Sibthorpiana.

CENTURIA PRIMA.

1806

MONS PARNASSUS.

The repercussions of the French Revolution had been widely felt in Greece. Furthermore, the decline of the Ottoman Empire and the disorganization of its central government were to prove favourable to the Greek cause. Already in the early years of the nineteenth century a new sense of national identity had emerged in Greece, which played a catalytic role in the mounting of a co-ordinated insurrection. The nominal independence of the Ionian Islands in 1814 served as an encouragement to the Greeks of the mainland.[31] The same year, the Philiki Etairia, a secret society dedicated to the formation of a large Greek-dominated state, was established in Odessa. Six years after its foundation the members of the Etairia attempted to secure as their leader Count Ioannes Capodistrias, who, although a Greek, was one of the most important ministers of the Tsar. When he refused, the leadership of the organization was assumed by Alexandros Ypsilantis, a Phanariot Greek and a general in the Russian army. The rising broke out early in March 1821. Ypsilantis invaded the principalities across the River Pruth, but found little sympathy for the Greek cause there, and the operation was unsuccessful. However, on 25 March, Germanos, the Metropolite of Patras, proclaimed the rising in the Peloponnesus and the revolt spread simultaneously over the Greek mainland and the islands.

This is the age of the war of the oppressed against the oppressors, and every one of those ringleaders of the privileged gangs of murderers and swindlers, called Sovereigns, look to each other for aid against the common enemy, and suspend their mutual jealousies in the presence of a mightier fear. Of this holy alliance all the despots of the earth are virtual members. But a new race has arisen throughout Europe, nursed in the abhorrence of the opinions which are its chains, and she will continue to produce fresh generations to accomplish that destiny which tyrants foresee and dread.

Thus wrote Shelley in the introduction to *Hellas* in 1822. In the 1820s the prevailing general intoxication with newly-evolved notions of freedom and emancipation – which were also programmes for action for Romantic revolutionaries of all nationalities – found expression, as far as Greece was concerned, in the Philhellenic movement.[32] Philhellenism created a new current of European opinion about Greece which ran counter to the policies of most governments.

As the news of the Greek uprising spread in Europe, a mass of volunteers appeared, eager to join the cause. The European supporters of an independent Greece included ex-soldiers, mercenaries, professional revolutionaries, political refugees, university graduates, run-away students, romantics and adventurers from all classes. A few months after the massacres of Scio in 1822, the Batallion of Philhellenes was organized. At the end of the same year the German Legion arrived in Greece. Throughout Europe Philhellenic Societies and Committees were formed in order to raise funds and recruit volunteers for the Greek cause: the London Greek Committee was founded in 1823; the Paris Greek Committee two years later. Byron's arrival on the scene transformed the Philhellenic movement into a Romantic crusade. His death in Greece in 1824 became a symbolic event and it led to a further intensification of Philhellenic feeling and activity. The destruction of Missolonghi, two years later, marked the climax of Philhellenic sentiments all over Europe.

'Will our century watch hordes of savages extinguish civilization at its rebirth on the tomb of a people who civilized the world? Will Christendom calmly allow Turks to strangle Christians? And will the Legitimate Monarchs of

H.L.V.J.B. Aubry-Lecomte,
*Chateaubriand and Mme de Staël
among the Greeks*, 1827

Europe shamelessly permit their sacred name to be given a tyranny which
could have reddened the Tiber?', wrote Chateaubriand in his *Note sur la Grèce*
(1825). Chateaubriand's statement aptly exemplifies the different aspects of
Philhellenism. Indeed, the Greek cause became equally the cause of Liberals, of
Christians, of humanists and of classical scholars, the cause of every honest
person in Europe. All members of the British Parliament that belonged to the
London Greek Committee were Whigs or Radicals, and Jeremy Bentham's name
figured in the original list of members of the Committee. The first French
society in favour of the Greeks was the 'Société de la morale chrétienne', a
philanthropic organization that was devoted to social reform. The Paris
Committee was largely composed of Liberals and Orleanists. In Germany the
most ardent sympathizers were to be found among liberal students, but it was
their professors who had originally put themselves at the head of the
Philhellenic movement. In 1825 the commander of the Greek Regular Forces
was Colonel Fabvier, an ex-officer of Napoleon devoted to the cause of
Liberalism. The same year the Conte di Santa Rosa, a famous *carbonaro* and one
of the leaders of the Piedmont revolution, was killed in Greece as a simple
soldier.

The Greek struggle also became the sacred war of the Christians against the
Infidels. Indeed, it recalled the Crusades in its juxtaposition between the Cross
and the Crescent. 'If our voice could be heard, the Standard of the Cross would
fly over the roofs of Constantinople or over the Parthenon, and the Church of
St Sophia would soon be restored to its former use,' proclaimed the
Constitutionnel on 26 July 1821. As well as being the descendants of Pericles,

the Greeks were also seen now as the descendants of the congregation of St Paul. The British Philhellene Edward Blaquiere confessed that he was helping the Greeks because he was 'enthusiastically favoured to Grecian freedom, not less from a sense of religion than of gratitude to their ancestors'. But European feelings of affection towards Greece were also fuelled by admiration for ancient Hellas. 'Europe has an enormous debt towards Greece . . . it is to Greece that it owes the arts and sciences,' declared Crown Prince Ludwig of Bavaria. Classical allusion was a common formula in Philhellenic literature and art. Lecturing on Racine's *Iphigénie*, Abel François Villemain told his audience: 'The Iphigenias of modern Greece are those Christian virgins who kill themselves rather than surrender. On their tombs we will mark the name Callimartyrs.' From Spain, Francisco Martínez de la Rosa incited the Greeks with the following verses:

> *Noble children of Sparta and Athens*
> *Listen to the voice of your country*
> *Break the shameful chains*
> *And forge the arms of the struggle.*[33]

Once again the light of Hellas shone upon the face of Greece; only this time the leaders of the Revolution attempted to use it for their country's sake.

Let us recollect, brave and generous Greeks, the liberty of the classic land of Greece, the battles of Marathon and Thermopylae; let us combat upon the tombs of our ancestors who, to leave us free, fought and died. The blood of our tyrants is dear to the shades of the Theban Epaminondas, and of the Athenian Thrasybulus . . . to those of Harmodius and Aristogiton . . . above all, to those of Miltiades, Themistocles, Leonidas, and the three hundred who massacred so many times their number of the innumerable army of the barbarous Persians – the hour is come to destroy their successors, more barbarous and still more detestable!

Such was the text of the Proclamation issued by Alexandros Ypsilantis in 1821.[34] The leaders of the Greek Revolution realized the benefits that would arise from the exploitation of their Hellenic heritage. Indeed, this emphasis on the affinities between Greeks and Hellenes not only made the Greek cause more attractive in the eyes of Europe, it also accentuated the growing sense of national identity felt by the Greeks themselves. Moreover, it seemed totally justifiable for the Greeks to lay claim to the world of Hellas as their motherland when the rest of Europe was doing the same. 'We are all Greeks . . . our laws, our literature, our religion, our arts have their roots in Greece,' declared Shelley in the preface to *Hellas*. Thus the Hellenic tradition that had been fostered in Europe was returned to Greece.

'It is not the governments of Europe who have saved Greece, but public opinion.' This statement is no exaggeration for Philhellenism was above all a great popular movement. The Greek cause appealed equally to French workers, Swiss bankers, ladies of the French aristocracy, German intellectuals, the royal family of Sweden, the Crown Prince of Bavaria – to every lofty-minded European. Philhellenism became a fashion, a sensation. Throughout Europe, literature on Greece poured off the presses; charity concerts were organized; plays were performed in aid of the *pallikars*; and exhibitions of pictures were held.

Wilhelm Müller's *Lieder der Griechen* (Songs of the Greeks), published in 1821, sold over a thousand copies in six weeks. The *Morgenblatt* of 1821 printed moving poems by Friederike Brün, Louise Brachmann and Amalie von Helvig-Imhoff. In Karl Iken's *Hellenion, über Kultur, Geschichte und Literatur der Neugriechen* (Hellenion: On the Culture, History and Art of the Modern Greeks), published in early 1822, German readers found a panoramic survey of Greece on the eve of the Revolution. A few months later, in England, 'The Tears of Scio', a poem in the *Morning Chronicle*, brought tears to the eyes of its readers. Among the elegies in Casimir Delavigne's collection *Messéniennes* (1818), the 'Tyrtée aux Grecs' and 'Aux ruines de la Grèce' touched the hearts of all. Alphonse de Lamartine adjured the god of war to fight with the Greeks in his poem 'Invocation pour les Grecs' (1826). Michel Pichat's tragedy *Léonidas* was enthusiastically received in 1825, and the presence of the son of the naval hero Kanaris in the box of the Duc d'Orléans added to the enthusiasm of the spectators. Rossini's opera *Le Siège de Corinthe*, with libretto by Alexandre Soumet, was also performed that year, After the fall of Missolonghi, Victor Hugo joined the ranks of the Philhellenes with his poem 'Les Têtes du Sérail' (1826).

The Greek struggle was, understandably, appropriated by painters as much as by writers. When reviewing the pictures on Greek themes exhibited at the Salon of 1827, a French art critic commented:

Happy are the people who hold a small place in history; happy are those who have never attracted the eyes of the poets and the artists. The monotonous existence of a peaceful nation provides none of the vivid and ardent sensations sought by genius. Those nations so often celebrated by the lyre or the pen have to pay for their fame by their happiness. And nowadays, with what price of blood and tears has Greece gained the right to inspire all the children of the Muses. The Hellenes, their heroism, their disasters, their victories, their defeats, have provided a mass of subjects for our painters.[35]

Pictorially, the heroic, religious, classical and oriental elements in the Greek wars offered European artists particularly sensational subject-matter. Furthermore, the subject was so familiar to the European public that artists made use of it in order to allude indirectly to the oppression in their own countries.

Philhellenic subjects were most popular with French painters. At the Galerie Lebrun in 1826 an exhibition was held 'au profit des Grecs'.[36] The names of the most eminent artists figured amongst the 198 works exhibited: Horace Vernet, A. M. Colin, Ary Scheffer A. Devéria, R. P. Bonington and Delacroix, who showed four works including *The Massacre of Scio*. Delacroix is considered to be the European Philhellenic artist *par excellence*. His *Massacre of Scio* was the only Greek war subject to be exhibited in the Salon of 1824,[37] and it presented Europeans for the first time with a Greek setting which was neither paradisiacally calm nor artificially dramatic. This time, the gloomy sky did not serve the purpose of inciting the spectator to melancholy comment on the transience of ancient glory. The fierce landscape with the air filled with smoke and fire were not merely effects of light – they were real.

'Rappelle-toi, pour t'enflammer éternellement, certains passages de Byron,' Delacroix noted in his diary on 11 May 1824. It was through Byron's verses that Greece was revealed to Delacroix, as it was to many of his contemporaries who painted Greek subjects. Byron had succeeded in blending the vibrant colour and mystery of the East with actuality. The dramatic and fatal heroes

Eugène Delacroix, *A Mounted Greek Warrior*, 1856

and heroines presented in *The Corsair*, *The Giaour*, *The Bride of Abydos* and *Don Juan* revealed a colourful and phantasmagoric world. If Byron's poetry satisfied the orientalist taste of the period, his role as the poetic champion of Greece and his death at Missolonghi stimulated a whole range of Greek iconography. Byron's maids and Suliote *pallikars* replaced classical nymphs and river-gods in the exhibition rooms, and the places associated with his poems became as attractive as the classical sites. The name of Missolonghi came to symbolize the aspirations of all European sympathizers with the Greek cause. While at the turn of the century Greece was depicted as a woman in classical dress, lying amongst the tombs of ancient heroes (as in the frontispiece of Choiseul-Gouffier's book) or lamenting at the foot of the Acropolis (as in J. M. W. Turner's fantasy), in 1827 modern Greece is expiring at Missolonghi. She no longer wears a tunic, and there is not a classical temple in sight. In the words of Sir Walter Scott:

p. 43
Pl. VII

> Greece, the cradle of poetry with which our earliest studies are familiar, was presented to us (by Lord Byron) among her ruins and her sorrows. Her delightful scenery, once dedicated to those deities who, though dethroned from their own Olympus, still preserve a poetical empire, was spread before us in Lord Byron's poetry, varied by all the moral effect derived from what Greece is, and what she has been; while it was doubted by comparisons, perpetually excited, between the philosophers and heroes who formerly inhabited the romantic country, and their descendants, who either stoop to their Scythian conquerors, or maintain among their classical mountains, an independence as wild and savage as it is precarious.

Louis Dupré, *Landscape with a
Greek*, *c.* 1830

Antoine Charles Horace Vernet, *The
Defeat*, 1827

Richard Parkes Bonington, *Portrait
of a Young Greek*, *c.* 1825–6

Karl Krazeisen, *Greeks Fighting among Classical Ruins*, 1829

Bronze ink-stand with a statuette of Markos Botsaris dying, *c.* 1835–40

Louis Dupré, *The Virgin of Thyamis*, 1825

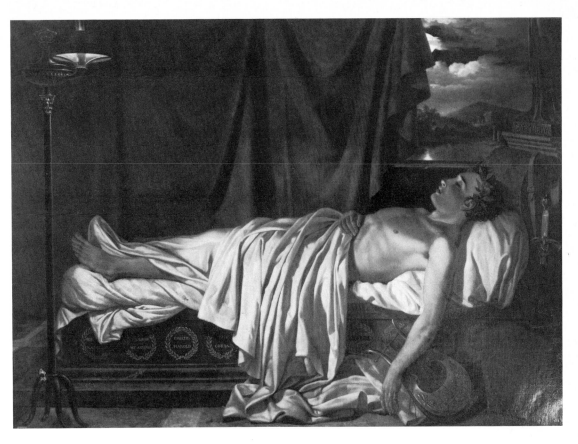

Joseph Denis Odevaere, *The Death of Byron*, 1826

This is not to say that classical allusions disappeared from Greek war imagery altogether: they were now broadly used, but in a new context. Now, they were allusions to the classical heritage which was a moving force for the Greeks and which they defended with a heroism worthy of their ancestors. In Karl Krazeisen's *Greeks Fighting among Classical Ruins* Greek warriors fight proudly under the Doric columns. In the French ink-stand depicting the dying figure of Markos Botsaris, that popular hero, a modern Leonidas, is expiring with the same dignity as the famous Hellenistic sculpture in the Museo Capitolino. In Joseph Odevaere's *Death of Byron* the poet's death-bed is placed under the statue of Liberty, his sword is leaning against the base of the statue, 'the lyre has escaped from the hands of the Bard of the Hellenes'. The expression of perfect tranquillity in Byron's face and his laurel-crowned head bring to mind the head of Hector in David's *Andromache Mourning the Death of Hector* (1783). Using a classical vocabulary, Odevaere has elevated the precise event into an image of universal significance. Nonetheless, the religious resonance of the Greek cause was now as powerful as the classical. The struggle between Cross and Crescent gave rise to such scenes as Dupré's *The Virgin of Thyamis*. 'This is how the infamous Turks mark their presence and their contempt for the Christian religion. When considering that there have been so many similar outrageous acts on one side, and so much suffering on the other, one begins to wonder if there are more Muslim powers in Europe than Christian,' Dupré declared.[38] Scenes of Last Communions, ferocious Turks eager to rape Christian virgins, and venerable priests being humiliated, fired the soul of Christian Europe.

Lodovico Lipparini, *Byron's Oath at Missolonghi*, 1824

Ary Scheffer, *A Young Greek Defending his Wounded Father*, 1827

Cesare dell'Acqua, *A Greek Mother*, 1860

Certainly, Romantic artists were moved more by the tragedies of the Revolution than by its achievements. It was usually the failures of the Greeks they depicted – such as *The Massacre of Scio*, *The Destruction of Missolonghi*, *The Sacrifice of the Suliote Women*, *The Evacuation of Parga* – rather than their victories. Most Philhellenic pictures reveal the artists' concern for emotional effect. Lodovico Lipparini's *Oath of Byron*, for instance, is as convincing emotionally as it is historically in its recreation of a heroic gesture in terms of everyday experience. The artist's wish is that such an event be instructive and morally improving – as is indicated by the old man's gesture to his grandson. In Ary Scheffer's *A Young Greek Defending his Wounded Father* the historical moment is intertwined with a personal drama, emphasizing both patriotism and moral virtue. The artist attempts to render the bravery and ethos of the boy who, despite his youth, realizes his sense of duty in the course of a desperate moment. Its message is that for a Greek to fight for his father and for freedom are the same thing. Such a scene not only moved the heart, but also sanctified the Greek cause. Cesare dell'Acqua's *Greek Mother* is a scene full of drama and emotion. Frightened yet fierce, the young mother leaves the spectator in no doubt that no enemy will ever take her child from her arms. A very successful Greek theme was the *Combat of the Giaour and the Pasha*.[39] Pictorially phantasmagoric, it was an explicit statement which also embodied a series of romantic suggestions. The contrast between Greek and Turk was seen equally as the struggle between Christianity and the Infidel, between Civilization and Barbarism, between Liberty and Oppression.

Ludwig Vogel, *Portraits of the Greek Refugees in Zürich*, 1823

Giovanni Boggi, *Portrait of Theodoros Kolokotronis*, 1825

Adam Friedel von Friedelsburg, *Portrait of Lascarina Bouboulina*, 1827

The most popular Greek subjects were lithographed and became widely known. In 1823 Ludwig Vogel was asked to execute the portraits of the Greek refugees from Ypsilantis's army in Zürich by the Swiss Philhellenic Committee who intended to have them lithographed and sold in aid of the Greeks. Giovanni Boggi's collection of the most famous characters in the Greek War was published between 1826 and 1829, while Adam Friedel's *Portraits of the Heroes of the Greek Revolution* appeared in London in 1827. Although drawn from life, most often these portraits bore little resemblance to reality. Indeed, it would have been impossible for even the least informed spectator to admit that 'Bobolina, The distinguished Heroine from Spezia' could have borne any similarity to Friedel's honey-trickling lady. In 1828 Jean Zuber's wallpaper factory in Rixheim issued a set of panoramic papers entitled 'Vues de la Grèce moderne ou les combats des Grecs'. The compositions, which were drawn by Jean Julien Deltil, were a pastiche of the most popular Greek scenes of the day.[40] Philhellenic pots, plates, firescreens and fans with representations of wounded *pallikars* and Athenian maids were sold in charity bazaars; a jeweller in Paris sold, 'au profit des Grecs', brooches in the shape and colours of the Greek flag; in Magdeburg a confectioner was selling cakes decorated with Philhellenic couplets. Philhellenic posters showing Lord Byron waving farewell to England and embarking for Greece were to be found all over Europe. French workers contributed money to the Revolution while saying, philosophically, 'The Greeks are French. Let us do one more good thing and drink one bottle less.' There were also depictions of aristocratic ladies giving away their jewellery in aid of the Greeks. The Greek struggles presented artists with unlimited material for often trivial scenes. In the lithographed series of 'The Dying Greek Warrior' or 'The Greek Warrior's Last Struggle' many of the unfortunate Greeks are depicted expiring in the most graceful postures: the taste for such operatically sentimental scenes knew no bounds. Nonetheless, such works served to keep Greece in the forefront of European public opinion.

BOBOLINA

The distinguished Heroine from Spezia | *Une Héroïne distinguée du l'Isle de Spezzia*

This Print forms one of the Series of Greek Portraits, 1st Part, | Publié a Londres et à Paris 1827, par A Friedel
now in course of Publication in London & Paris 1827 by A Friedel | Ces dessins forment une Serie de Portraits des Grecs, 1er Partie,
& Sold by the principal Book & Printsellers in Town & Country | et se trouve chez tous les principaux libraires et marchan
 | d'estampes à Paris et dans les departements.

Bronze clock decorated with a
statuette of Konstantinos Kanaris,
c. 1835–40

Bronze clock decorated with a
scene from the Greek War of
Independence, *c.* 1825–30

Porcelain vase representing the
'Battle of the Giaour and the Pasha'

Porcelain plate representing the
French Philhellenic Committee,
c. 1830

Music score, 'Le dernier cri des
Grecs', 1828

The Defeat. Firescreen after the
painting by Antoine Charles Horace
Vernet (see also p. 51)

George Philip Reinagle, *The Battle
of Navarino*, 1827

George Cruickshank, *The Luncheon
of the Great Powers after the Battle
of Navarino*, 1827

Although at the beginning of the Revolution the Greeks had hoped that official Europe would bless their enterprise, throughout the years of their struggle mutual distrust between the Great Powers frustrated a number of tentative interventionist proposals. However, the landing of the Egyptian troops under Ibrahim Pasha in the Morea in 1824 forced a change of policy upon them. The Great Powers recognized that if there was to be any stability in the Eastern Mediterranean, collective action was needed. In April 1826 an Anglo-Russian protocol was signed, by which the two Powers agreed on British mediation between the Turks and the Greeks with the object of making Greece an autonomous vassal state of the Ottoman Empire. When at the end of that year the two Powers asked Austria, Prussia and France to share in the peace-making in Greece, only France accepted the invitation. On 6 July 1827 the three governments concluded the Treaty of London and their naval commanders in the Mediterranean were ordered to cut off supplies from Egypt. The Battle of Navarino, that 'untoward event', as the Duke of Wellington described it, took place on 10 October, and ended with the total defeat of the Ottoman fleet. It also caused great embarrassment to the English, and aroused strong reactions in the capitals of Europe.[41] Nonetheless, public opinion was delighted, and new sets of Greek prints filled the shop windows. Within a few weeks illustrations and descriptions of the scene appeared in France and in England. A. L. Garneray made a sketch-map of the battle and several paintings; G. P. Reinagle, an eye-witness of the event, collected enough material to publish a folio with lithographic representations of the battle and to exhibit Navarino scenes from 1829 to 1831. Masses of people gathered in the Panorama of the 'Battle of Navarin' exhibited by Robert Burford in the Strand in 1828. In Paris Charles Langlois also exhibited a panorama of the battle in 1831. Seventeen works with Greek subjects were exhibited in the Salon of 1827;[42] subscribing to the general feeling of enthusiasm, the French Academy in the same year chose 'L'Indépendance de la Grèce' as the subject for the prize in poetry.

A year after the Battle of Navarino the Great Powers decided to enforce the evacuation of the Peloponnesus by the Egyptian forces under the command of Ibrahim Pasha. The French army undertook the task, and on 30 August 1828 an army of 14,000 men under the command of General Maison landed at Petalidi. With the Morea expedition France aimed to secure a dynamic presence in the East and to demonstrate to both European and Greek public opinion its decisive contribution to the liberation of Greece. Within a month of the French army's arrival, the Egyptian troops had evacuated the area. But the expedition also

served another purpose. In the spring of 1828 a group of French scientists had arrived in Greece with the intention of studying the topography, flora, archaeology and architecture of the Peloponnesus in the same way as the Scientific Expedition to Egypt. The members of the expedition were naturalists, mineralogists, engineers, geographers, classical scholars, archaeologists and architects. The work of the French expedition to the Peloponnesus was remarkable.[43] For the first time systematic excavations were carried out, and the most detailed topographical maps drawn up. The survey was supplemented by statistical studies of the population and most of the members of the expedition kept notes on the everyday features of the area, and on the customs and costumes of its people. The results of this monumental survey appeared in three richly illustrated volumes between 1831 and 1838 under the title *Expédition scientifique de Morée*. When they returned to France, however, the scientists took with them all the sculptures they had discovered in their excavations of the Temple of Zeus at Olympia.

The Battle of Navarino enormously strengthened the position of the Greeks, even though it did not resolve their problems. The Greek National Assembly at Troezene in March 1828 drafted a new constitution and elected Count Capodistrias as President. Capodistrias's immediate task was to negotiate with the Great Powers for as large a Greek state as possible. On 22 March 1829 an Anglo-Franco-Russian protocol drew the frontiers of the new Greek state from just south of the Gulf of Arta, on the west, to the Gulf of Volo on the Aegean coast, excluding the islands of Samos and Crete. The Powers also nominated Leopold of Saxe-Coburg as ruler of the country, but he declined the offer. The assassination of Capodistrias in October 1831 was followed by a period of chaos in the new state. Four months later the Great Powers agreed on Prince Otho, the seventeen-year-old son of King Ludwig I of Bavaria, as ruler of Greece, an independent and monarchical state, under the guarantee of the three Powers. On 6 February 1833 King Otho landed at Nafplion accompanied by the three Bavarian Regents[44] who were to govern until he himself came of age.

The picturesque compromise

THE NEW Greek state embraced within its frontiers only about half of the Greek population. Thessaly, Epirus and Macedonia were excluded, as were Crete and most of the islands except those immediately adjacent to the mainland. Nor were any of the important centres of Greek commerce in the Ottoman Empire included in the new state, and Greece had to pay an indemnity to the Porte. Until the young king came of age, the country was to be ruled by three Bavarian Regents, Count Joseph von Armansberg, Professor Ludwig von Maurer and Major-General Karl Wilhelm von Heydeck.[1] Although there was no written constitution as such, there was a civil service, and order was maintained by an army of 5,000 troops recruited in Bavaria. The educational system was based on German and French models for, as Maurer had declared, 'just as the Greeks in the fourteenth and fifteenth centuries brought wisdom to the rest of Europe, so now Europeans, especially the Germans, must return the light to the land from which it has long since vanished'.[2]

In keeping with this idea of returning the light to its homeland, it was decided that the capital of the new kingdom should be moved to Athens. Thus, on 1 December 1834, King Otho made his public entry into the capital of Greece:

> King Otho disembarked from a Greek vessel of war at the Piraeus, under a salute of twenty-one guns. The regency . . . accompanied by . . . the ministers of the interior and foreign affairs . . . the nomarch of Athens, and . . . all the municipality of the town, received his Majesty upon landing.
>
> As the procession moved towards the town, the cavalcade increased, being joined by several who were hastening to the Piraeus to pay their devoirs to royalty. All the Greek old warriors were there, with General Church at their head; and these celebrated men added much to the scene . . .
>
> Near to the temple of Theseus there is an archway leading to one of the principal streets of the town. Round this arch were placed branches of laurel and olive, and under it his Majesty entered to the new capital of his dominions. Just before you arrive at this portico, there is a rise in the ground, and upon this about five thousand Athenians, with their wives and children, had placed themselves to welcome the young monarch, who received their acclamations with much grace.
>
> His majesty, having passed with his suite through the tortuous streets of his new capital, arrived at his temporary residence, – a very humble one, composed of about twelve rooms, a quarter of a mile out of the town.[3]

The challenge of presiding over the creation of a new Hellenic state excited the young king and, in May 1834, a Government Archaeological Department was set up. In August that year, in the presence of Otho, the symbolic restoration of the Parthenon was begun. Leo von Klenze, who supervised the first stage of the restoration, addressed Otho in the following words:

[When the works began] the shadows of those great spirits who until then had suspected their imminent destruction in any stroke of an axe or the sound of workers' voices, rose from their peaceful tombs and raised their arms above these exalted ruins as if trying to protect them. Thus everything was against our operations. The levers broke, the workers fell ill, the masons believed that the works ought to be suspended. But O!, the blue flag of hope appeared on the distant horizon: the king was coming with his counsellors in order to undertake the work of rescue . . . and, as if by miracle,

63

Karl Friedrich von Schinkel, *Project for a Royal Palace on the Acropolis*, 1834

those gigantic marbles began to obey the masons and harmonize under the sound of the hymns that saluted the king.[4]

The Muses were to be returned to Hellas: this the Bavarians held in firm belief. The eminent archaeologist Ludwig Ross was appointed Director of the Archaeological Department during 1834–6 where he began to prepare a systematic survey of all archaeological sites.[5] The archaeological task was made easier by the arrival of foreign architects in liberated Greece from the late 1820s onwards:[6] Eduard Schaubert in 1828; Christian Hansen and F. Stauffert in 1833; and Hansen's brother, Theophil, in 1838. Plans were drawn up for the rebuilding of Nafplion, Patras, Argos, Sparta, Chalcis and Hermoupolis; while the German Eduard Schaubert and the Greek Stamatios Kleanthis drew up a grandiose plan for the new Athens (later simplified by Leo von Klenze).

To transform Athens, then no more than a 'heap of ruins', into a European capital was a major challenge. In 1834 Karl Friedrich Schinkel submitted to Otho a spectacular scheme for a royal palace on the Acropolis incorporating the ancient structures. This 'Midsummer Night's Dream', as Klenze called it, was, thankfully, later abandoned in favour of the more modest effort of Friedrich von Gaertner (erected 1836–40). Athens became a hive of architectural activity. The so-called Athenian Trilogy – the Academy, University and National Library – was built between 1838 and 1888 by Christian and Theophil Hansen. The latter also executed the plans for the Observatory (1843–6). The Military Hospital was built in 1836 by Wilhelm von Weiler; and Ludwig Lange made the designs for the Archaeological Museum (not finally completed until 1866). The Elementary School of Drawing, opened in 1836, had an international staff: Ludwig Lange was Teacher of Drawing; Charles Laurent, of Architecture; and Pierre Bonirote, of Painting.

Otho's enthronement gave rise to a whole iconography. Peter von Hess, who accompanied Otho to Greece, was commissioned by Ludwig of Bavaria to record the king's arrival and to execute a series of historical scenes from the War of Independence. In Munich, the famous lithographer Johann L. Rugendas was selling a series of prints of the most popular subjects connected with Otho's progress.

Peter von Hess, *King Otho's Arrival in Nafplion on 6 February 1833, 1839*

Peter von Hess, *King Otho Received by the Greek Patriarch at the Theseum on 13 January 1835, 1835*

Alexandre Marie Colin, *Landscape with a Greek Boy*, 1831

A Young Greek Defending his Wounded Father. Tapestry panel after the painting by Ary Scheffer (see also p. 54)

While historical scenes and portraits of the heroes of the Revolution continued to attract artists, in many cases they were used merely as an excuse for studies of foreign costumes and miscellaneous exotica. In A. M. Colin's *Landscape with a Greek Boy* a beautifully dressed boy is surrounded by piles of muskets and swords that are far too big for him and make him look like a toy soldier. Sir Charles Lock Eastlake's picture of *Greek Fugitives* also seems to explore these same possibilities, although the artist's main concern was to praise the British role in Greek affairs: according to Finden's description in his *Gallery of British Art*, 'the picture may be considered to represent an episode of that devastating war, in which, driven from their hearths, the unfortunate Greeks sometimes found safety on board the British ships stationed on the coast, and which were on the watch to succour them'. Exhibited at the Royal Academy in 1833, the year of the proclamation of the new Greek kingdom, the painting touched the hearts of English spectators. Of course, the Greek struggle was no longer a contemporary event and, as memory dimmed, representations became stereotyped and mannered. In the 1830s Greek heroes were aged. Lipparini's picture of the *Old Warrior* is quite effective with its sentimental overtones: the warrior, seated on a broken column and looking over his shoulder, still clasps his sword tightly. But in Ludwig Köllnberger's *Interior of the 'Orea Hellas'* the *pallikars* are depicted as clients in a fashionable coffee-house; and the tapestry panel after Ary Scheffer's *Young Greek Defending his Wounded Father* is a striking example of the trivialization of a heroic theme.

p. 70

66

Charles Lock Eastlake, *Greek Fugitives*, 1833

Lodovico Lipparini, *An Old Greek Warrior*, 1842

Many artists visited Greece during Otho's reign with official commissions. In 1833, for example, Johann Michael Wittmer accompanied Otho's brother Maximilian when he visited Greece. In November 1840 three German artists, Ulrich Halbreiter, Joseph Kranzberger and Claudius von Schrandolph, were sent to Athens to execute the frieze designed by Ludwig Michael von Schwanthaler for the Hall of the Trophies in the royal palace. In 1842 the team was joined by Joseph Scherer, Thomas Guggenberger and Franz Joseph Vourm.

Buildings in Athens sprang up like mushrooms. As a traveller of 1850 remarked: 'There is nothing particularly Greek in the physiognomy of Athens. The houses of the better sort are German in outward appearance, while the poorer dwellings resemble those of the Italian villages. A few squat, ancient churches, which have a mellow flavor of the Lower Empire, remain here and there, and the new ones are likewise Byzantine, but of a plainer and less picturesque stamp.'[7] Julie von Nordenflycht, one of the queen's ladies-in-waiting, wrote: 'It may be considered a heroic act to wander through Athens on four wheels; every street is filled with stones and building materials, while the streets are so narrow that it is impossible to turn.'[8]

All artists attested to the striking contrasts not only in architecture, but also in costume (fustanellas *and* redingotes), in life style, and in manners and ideas. And it certainly made for a picturesqueness that delighted them. W. H. Bartlett, for example, comments on the introduction of European elements into Greek life: 'among other signs of improvement was a rank of crazy-looking vehicles intended to imitate our cabs; but instead of a sullen fellow, in a dirty mackintosh, the driver was a "gay and gilded Greek" in a red jacket and cap and white petticoat and leggings'.[9] Greece in the mid-nineteenth century provided, in fact, a whole range of features from the picturesque repertoire. Pl. 45 The contents of *An Athenian Quarter* by J. P. E. F. Peytier, for instance, are like an advertisement for the picturesque possibilities that Greece afforded: in the foreground are some medieval ruins crowned with weeds; further on, a group of colourfully dressed Greeks are seated among ancient ruins; then there is a palm tree and, in the distance, a classical temple (the Theseum) surrounded by modern houses – a perfect stage-setting. A similar theme is taken up in Ippolito Caffi's *Agora Gate*, as well as in J. N. H. de Chacaton's *Hadrian's Library*.

Pls 42, XX

In William Cole's illustrations to *Remains of Ancient Monuments in Greece*, published in 1835, while it is the classical monuments that claim the artist's attention, these are seen more as familiar pictorial motifs than as objects of study; in Christian Perlberg's *Fête by the Olympieum* the columns of the temple are imposing, yet are deprived of their significance by the figures in the foreground; and John Linton, in his *Shepherd and Shepherdess*, has created a truly intimate scene despite the use of classical motifs. Indeed, the classical ruins of Greece were now viewed more as curiosities by European lovers of the picturesque. In 1851 the architect Henry Cook published a series of articles in the *Art Journal* entitled 'The Present State of the Monuments of Greece' in which he argued for the conservation of the ancient monuments without any further restoration for the sake of their picturesque qualities:

Pl. VI

I think the feeling which at present reigns for the restoration of ruins, the classification of fragments . . . should be cried down by the united protest of all real lovers of the picturesque. Why, I know not, but certain I am that the Parthenon as it now stands, a ruin in every sense of the term, its walls destroyed, its columns shivered, its friezes scattered, its capitals half-buried by their own weight – but clear of all else, is, if not a grander, assuredly a more impressive object than when, in the palmiest days of Athenian glory, its marble . . . first met the rays of the morning sun.[10]

European artists hurried to fill their portfolios with more alluring material for clients who were now getting tired of deserted classical landscapes. Joseph Scherer, for instance, who was in Greece in 1842–4, specialized in the people and their costumes. In his sketches of street scenes every detail of the costume

John Linton, *Shepherd and Shepherdess*, c. 1850

Ludwig Köllnberger, *The Famous Athenian Coffee-house 'Orea Hellas',* 1837

embroideries is captured. Richard Dadd, who paid a brief visit to Greece in 1842, was also fascinated by the people. 'I never saw such an assemblage of deliciously villainous faces,' he noted in his diary; 'Oh! such heads! enough to turn the brain of an artist.'

The many illustrated travel-books on Greece published at this time provided their readers with appropriately pictorial specimens of a country with Eastern manners and Western architecture, sunny shores, classical temples and European facilities for travel. In 1837 Francis Hervé published an illustrated two-volume account of his Greek tour entitled *A Residence in Greece and Turkey.* Ten years later the *Voyage pittoresque en Grèce et dans le Levant* appeared, a richly illustrated edition of an extensive tour of the mainland and the islands by two Frenchmen, the draughtsman Etienne Rey and the architect A. M. Chenavard. The Swiss painter J. J. Wolfensberger was in Athens in 1834 collecting material for illustrations for such popular travel-books of the period as G. N. Wright's *The Rhine, Italy and Greece* (1840). Andrea Gasparini's collection of views in Athens drawn in 1843 consists of animated genre scenes. Théodore du Moncel's illustrations in his *De Venise à Constantinople* (1843) are faithfully studied. The main attraction of the plates in Edward Lear's *Journals of a Landscape Painter in Albania*, published in 1851, is the artist's genuine sensitivity in conveying the historical associations of each particular site connected with the recent events in Greece. Lear's folio of *Views in the Seven Ionian Islands*, published in 1863, is a remarkable document of the scenery of those islands.

A number of European artists during this period expressed a more Romantic approach to Greece. Less concerned with its picturesque aspects, they attempted to invest familiar scenes with an intensity that was suggestive of a personal dialogue. 'The remains of the buildings or temples . . . do not fit the artist's folio,' wrote William James Muller when he visited Greece in 1838.[11] To

Muller, the landscape painter was 'one who would delight in Nature, in her . . .
moods and beauties'. His *View of Salamis* conveys a sense of melancholy; in his   Pl. 70
View of Rhodes he seems more concerned to record his own experience of the   Pl. 77
place rather than indulge in mere map-making. 'What do I care about
Agamemnon and his empire? These ancient historical tales are of no interest to
the people of today, nor to reality,' declared Alphonse de Lamartine when
visiting Greece in 1834. 'I much prefer a tree, a spring under a rock or a laurel-
rose by the river's bank under the crumbling arch of a bridge, covered in ivy,
to the monuments of one of these ancient kingdoms, which strike no other
chord within me, other than the boredom which they instilled when I was a
child.'[12] T. H. Cromek's *Hill of the Areopagus* is at first sight a view of a familiar   Pl. 41
classical ruin, yet, by juxtaposing it against an indistinct landscape
background, the artist contrives to suggest a sense of loneliness. Edward Lear's
Rocks of Suli is an accurate topographical view, but it also expresses that   Pl. 6
overpowering sense of awe the artist felt there. Similarly, Karl Rottman's *View
of Santorini* manages to capture the atmosphere of the island.   Pl. XXVIII

Greece was also on the threshold of the Orient. Several European Orientalist
painters paid a hasty visit to Greece in the 1830s and 1840s: A. G. Decamps in
1827: Eugène Flandrin two years later; J. F. Lewis in 1840; and Horace Vernet
in 1843. They all spent some time – a few days, perhaps only a few hours – in
Corfu or Athens, and then hastened on to more exotic and colourful locations.
As Prosper Marilhat wrote to his sister from Athens in 1831: 'I am not saying
that Greece is a charming, cultivated, well-forested country . . . because I
would be lying if I did; but I am saying that it is a country . . . covered with
rocks that are arid but have imposing shapes, with desert-like plains that have
a grandeur and solemn beauty.'[13]

If in 1800 European artists had been concerned with the authentication of
classical myth and legend, by 1850 their interest had shifted towards the
authentication of Biblical topography. In fact, the revival of specifically
religious subject-matter in art, together with a new interest in Byzantine studies
throughout Europe, led to a revaluation of the surviving Byzantine monuments
in Greece which had been largely ignored until then. In his *Manuel
d'iconographie chrétienne, grecque et latine*, published in 1845, A. N. Didron
urged Ludwig of Bavaria to persuade Otho to put a stop to the pulling down of
Byzantine edifices within the classical sites of Greece. In 1855 Ludwig
Thiersch's Nazarene-style frescoes for the restored Byzantine church of Soteira
Lycodimou in Athens were highly acclaimed in the Greek press. Some years
later the artist Mary Hogarth wrote: 'The medieval churches [in Greece] stand
alone . . . to satisfy the craving of the historic sense for visible evidence of
continuity between past and present . . . The tired visitor will find that he
often returns from the shattered grandeurs of a dead past, or the imperfectly
realised pretensions of the . . . present.'[14]

Now that the Greeks had gained their freedom, European Christians began
to worry about the salvation of their souls. 'What a sight! What vivid
recollections!', the Reverend S. S. Wilson exclaimed when visiting Thebes.[15]
'*There*, Homer's chivalric bands had fought, and sinned and bled. *There*, many
a bard had sung, many a hero had multiplied widows and orphans . . . *There*,
inspired apostles had taught ''the glorious gospel'', and vanquished Apollo by
the simple story of the Cross.' Despite the failure of previous attempts by the

Catholic Church, the first English and American Protestant missionaries who arrived in Greece in 1828 aimed to contribute to the educational system by opening schools and publishing moral tracts. Yet their efforts too were on the whole unsuccessful since their presence aroused a cultural conflict with the clergy and traditionally-minded masses.

But the attraction of modern Greece was not to last. Where previously European travellers to Greece had praised these picturesque contrasts in manners and scenery, soon they began to find them grotesque. Greece no longer lived up to their expectations; in some way, they thought, the new, liberated Greece lied to its past. In his *Geschichte der Halbinsel Morea während des Mittelalters* (History of the Peninsula of the Morea in the Middle Ages), published in 1830, and his *Über die Entstehung der Neugriechen* (On the Origins of the Modern Greeks), published five years later, Professor J. F. Fallmerayer claimed that the Greeks were of Albanian and Slav descent 'with hardly a drop of Greek blood in their veins'. To the Comte d'Estourmel, in his *Journal d'un voyage en Orient*, published in 1844, Greece was a country of liars and thieves. Europeans discovered that the regeneration of Greece was a slow process. Visitors found the rich Greeks ridiculous in their aping of Western manners, while the sight of so many beggars in the streets made them wonder what had become of their 'good Philhellenic money'.

Moreover, Europeans loathed the political instability of Othonian Greece. As the Austrian ambassador Anton Prokesch von Osten stated: 'the government and the governed are like two people who have not been introduced to each other'. When, in November 1836, Otho married Amalia of Oldenburg, the Greeks only learned of the event through the European press. On 3 September 1843 a demonstration of large crowds and troops before the Palace demanded that the king concede a constitution, which was promulgated in March 1844.

'The Greeks for whom our mothers embroidered flags are not hospitable,' declared the French writer Edmond About, referring perhaps to the fact that after the 1844 Constitution all foreigners were excluded from public office. All the same, Europeans competed with each other for the role of patrons of the Greeks. The French hated the snobbish English 'Mylordi' who pretended to speak no other language but their own; the English loathed the idea of being in the same hotel with the noisy and pompous French; English and French hated the idea of Athens having become the 'capital of a petty German state'; and French, English and Germans were highly suspicious of the Orthodox Russians. While this foreign competition was encouraged by the Greeks because it seemed to serve as a guarantee against the political excesses of the various parties,[16] Europeans despised the Greeks for being equally obliging to all:

The feelings of the Greeks towards the nations of the West, and particularly towards their protectors, are not easy to unravel. The peasant, whom chance has brought in contact with a traveller, begins by asking whether he is French, Russian, German, or English, and, according to the answer, replies with an air of conviction, 'I very much like the French, they are so lively and generous'; or, 'I adore the Russians, they are Orthodox'; or, 'I venerate the Germans, they have given us the best of kings'; or, 'I have the greatest admiration for the English, they are as good sailors as we are'.[17]

The early 1840s were marked by nationalist movements throughout Greece which caused the continual intervention of the Great Powers in Greek affairs and made Greece very unpopular in Europe. At this time almost all Greeks

Ludwig Thiersch, *Portrait of a Greek Lady*, c. 1870

Gustave Doré, *Scene with Greek Bandits*. From Edmond About, *Le Roi des montagnes*, 5th edition, 1861

subscribed to what became known as the 'Megali Idea' (the Great Idea), the union of all unredeemed Greeks of the Ottoman Empire within a Greek state. 'There are two main centres of Hellenism: Athens, the capital of the Greek Kingdom . . . [and] ''The City'' [Constantinople], the dream and hope of all Greeks,' Prime Minister Kolettis declared in the Constituent Assembly in 1844.[18] During the Near Eastern crisis of 1839–40 the Cretans revolted, demanding *enosis* (union),[19] and the same claim was made by the northern territories of the mainland. The period 1848–9 also saw nationalist agitation in the Ionian Islands, to the great disapproval of Britain. The incident of Don Pacifico, a Maltese Jew and British subject, whose home had been plundered during anti-Jewish riots in Athens at Easter 1847, was turned into a major claim against the Greek government by Palmerston, who ordered a blockade of the Piraeus in January 1850. The dangers inherent in this situation were not lost on the artist Edward Lear, who was contemplating a tour of the mainland. As he wrote to his sister Ann from Corfu in 1849: 'Greece is at present a good deal excited . . . I rather incline to a tour in Albania.'[20]

British hostility towards the Greeks was shared by the French. When Russia exercised her right of protection over the Orthodox Christians of the Ottoman Empire and invaded the Danubian principalities, Britain and France declared war on Russia in March 1854 and occupied the Piraeus in order to secure Greece's neutrality. While the occupation, which lasted until February 1857, stimulated the resentment the Greeks felt towards their protectors, one of the most popular books in France and England during these same years was *La Grèce contemporaine* by Edmond About, published in 1854. About's impressions of his sojourn in Athens in 1851 as a member of the French Institute took the form of a libellous satire on the Greeks and on the Bavarian monarchy. Greek opinion, as expressed by the newspaper *Le Spectateur de l'Orient*, was that About was a hunchback jester who sought to divert Europe from her remorse for having neglected the Greeks. About's book abounds in critical comments about Greece. Some of the chapter-headings are quite explicit: 'Climate of Greece; intolerable heat and terrible cold – Greece lives in a state of bankruptcy from its birth – Justice: no justice – The Greeks are undisciplined and jealous – The men sleep in the streets and the women on the roofs – All the Greeks practise their religion but do not lead better lives for that – The King and the Queen have remained German: they love Greece as one loves a property – The King has not health enough: the Queen has too much –.' And elsewhere: 'The newspapers are about the whole of the literature of the country.'

Letters flooded *The Times* from enthusiastic readers who totally agreed with About. Some thought he was not critical enough because he did not stress one of the worst evils of the new Greek state, brigandage, which was endemic in Greece throughout Otho's reign. While the men of the hills, who maintained that they were revolting against Othonian oppression, were endowed by the Greeks with a certain savage nobility, nonetheless their ranks were constantly reinforced by outlaws of all kinds. Many travellers had fallen victim, but their loss was usually only a ransom. In 1857 About published a hilarious novel, *Le Roi des montagnes*, in which just such an incident is described culminating with the heroine threatening to complain to Lord Palmerston and to write to *The Times* urging that the Mediterranean fleet be dispatched to the Piraeus.

A series of revolts and diplomatic interventions led to Otho's deposition and deportation on 23 October 1862. The quest for a new sovereign started afresh, one of the most popular candidates being Prince Alfred, the second son of Queen Victoria. He had visited Greece as a midshipman in 1859 and had won all hearts. For the Greeks he was 'our Alfred', but for Queen Victoria his candidacy was out of the question. The Great Powers at last hit upon Prince Christian William Ferdinand Adolphus George, the eighteen-year-old son of the heir to the Danish throne. The fact that King George I was proclaimed King of the Hellenes, as opposed to 'King of Greece', delighted the Greeks as it implied that he was sovereign of all Greeks, not only of those presently within the boundaries of the Greek kingdom. In March 1864, a year after his proclamation, Britain ceded the Ionian Islands to Greece by treaty as a goodwill gesture.

But the change of dynasty did not do much to alter European feelings towards Greece. Visiting the country in 1867, Mark Twain remarked:

The Greek throne . . . went begging for a good while. It was offered to one of Victoria's sons, and afterwards to various other younger sons of royalty who had no thrones and were out of business, but they all had the charity to decline the drear honour, and veneration enough for Greece's ancient greatness to refuse to mock her sorrowful rags and dirt with a tinsel throne in this day of her humiliation – till they came to this young Danish George, and he took it . . . I suppose that ancient Greece and modern Greece compared, furnish the most extravagant contrast to be found in history. George I, an infant of eighteen, and a scraggy nest of foreign office holders, sit in the places of Themistocles, Pericles, and the illustrious scholars and generals of the Golden Age of Greece.[21]

In 1869 the Great Powers forced the Greeks to accede to their request to make no further incursions into European Turkish territory. But the following year unprecedented wrath was focused on Greece, because of the so-called Dilessi Murders.[22] Already in 1854 a European traveller to Greece had pointed out in a letter to *The Times* that 'whilst the robber in Europe adopts the formula of "Your money *or* your life", the Greek prefers "Your money *and* your life"'.

Gustave Doré, *Scene with Greek Bandits*. From Edmond About, *Le Roi des montagnes*, 5th edition, 1861

Unfortunately, this became true in the spring of 1870 when a party of three English aristocrats and an Italian count were murdered by brigands. Despite the distress of the Greeks themselves, public opinion in Europe came to the conclusion that Greece was a nest of robbers and a disgrace to civilization. The last decades of the nineteenth century in Greece were marked by revolutions and political disturbances. In 1880 Greece acquired Thessaly and half of Epirus, but when in 1885 it claimed the rest of Epirus another blockade of Greece by the Great Powers was mounted. Ironically, the commander of the British squadron was Prince Alfred, who had been one of the candidates for the Greek throne.

In the late nineteenth century contemporary Greece seemed finally to lose its attraction for European artists. But what of Hellas? In a period of rapid industrialization and shifting values the vision of ancient Hellas seemed to offer some hope of certainty. It was, perhaps, the one sure refuge. A new image of Greece now inspired European artists. If in the early nineteenth century artists had portrayed a Greece that was a timeless, rarefied, intellectual world, the Classicists of the late nineteenth century presented a spectacular realm of perpetual holidays. No longer concerned with appealing to the educated imagination, they provided the spectator with a highly-coloured reconstruction

Jean Léon Gérome, *The Atelier of Tanagra*, c. 1850

76

of daily life in ancient Greece. In the *Atelier of Tanagra*, for example, by J. L. Gérome, little is left to the spectator's imagination. Lured into a false sense of intimacy with the ancient Greeks, the spectator supposed that it was possible to enjoy such scenes fully without the aid of classical scholarship.

Lord Leighton, *Greek Girls Playing at Ball*, 1889

The pictorial world of these Classicists was moulded by such aesthetic principles as harmony, youth and brightness. Their use of bright colours was not unconnected with the discovery of the original polychromy of Greek sculpture. When the Crystal Palace was reopened at Sydenham in 1854, its Greek Court contained a vividly coloured cast of the Parthenon frieze. Besides, if youth was associated with innocence, then the Classicists were able to use pictorial subject-matter which would otherwise have shocked the public. Indeed, their naked Greek boys and girls in graceful amorous postures required an aesthetic justification for respectable eyes. Hiram Power's sculpture *The Greek Slave*, shown at the Great Exhibition of 1851, represented a Greek girl, naked, with her wrists chained, implying that she was destined for a Turkish harem. The erotic implications were obvious – and yet Elizabeth Barrett Browning composed a sonnet in praise of its 'passionless perfection'. Hellenic nudity was capable of purifying any naked figure in the eyes of prudish Victorians,[23] though some were reluctant to accept it. 'We seem to have infected the Greek ages themselves with the breath . . . of our hypocrisy,' John Ruskin declared,[24] although he himself was one of the victims of that hypocrisy.

This aesthetic conception of Hellenism encouraged artists to project their fantasies and aspirations in recreating scenes of extravagant theatricality peopled with handsome men and deliciously rounded women with Nereids' hair and 'classical' straight noses, attired in stylized draperies and depicted in frozen postures, surrounded by classical architecture with brilliantly polished surfaces. Such 'Hollywood' pictures as Lord Leighton's *Greek Girls Playing at* p. 77 *Ball* were, nevertheless, applauded as equivalent to the perished masterpieces of the most eminent painters in classical Greece, Polygnotus and Zeuxis.

Before the end of the nineteenth century, however, not only was classical imagery to be demythologized by such pictures as Edouard Manet's *Olympia*, but also the assumed universality of the classical world was put in question. Behind the rational façade of the classical world, it was now felt, there were also dark forces. 'Dionysus is a judge . . . there is the deepest experience of all Greeks', Nietzsche declared in 1887 in *The Will to Power*; 'We do not know the Greeks as long as this hidden and subterranean access to them remains obstructed.' And the excavations by Heinrich Schliemann at Mycenae and Tiryns during the late 1870s and 1880s revealed new aspects of Greek antiquity. The European image of ancient Greece could no longer be fitted into the accepted framework. Systematic excavations were undertaken by the European archaeological schools in Athens (the German Archaeological Institute was founded in 1874; the British School of Archaeology in 1885). More complex perspectives for the study of classical art and history were opened up in Europe, and the classical yardstick ceased to be the only measure of Greece's participation in European affairs.

In the preface to her *La Jeune Grèce*, published in 1897, Marie Anne de Bovet wrote: 'Modern Greece was expected to be built upon a naked present . . . with all the uncertainties of the character of a state that remains considerably oriental . . . yet also equipped with a legendary past, a glorious heritage of three thousand years. . . . Indeed, there are unbearable glories. Such is the glory of Greece.'

II · A journey through Greece

'One has to be familiar with the Greek atmosphere, the Greek sun and the character of the Greek soil to be able to imagine the beauty of this sight. The south of Italy, Calabria, Apulia and Sicily, cannot help us visualize these distant Greek landscapes in which the richest mountain-tops, comparable to statues of Phidias and Praxiteles carved with purity and plasticity, may vanish in a variety of colour with which nothing can be compared in terms of harmony, freedom, choice of hues and the playful changes of the light. Indeed, distant landscapes, chains of mountains and clustered rocks truly exist only in Greece, and even the Italian sky never has the infinite charm possessed by the Greek atmosphere, this luminous space which is so well described by the words "an ether of surpassing brightness".'

Leo von Klenze, *Aphoristische Bemerkungen gesammelt auf seiner Reise nach Griechenland*, 1838

MACEDONIA

EPIRUS

CHALCIDICE

△Athos

Salonica

△Olympus

Tempe

△Ossa

Ioannina

Meteora

THESSALY

MAGNESIA

Larissa

Corfu

CORFU

Suli

Parga

PAXOS

Pelion

Portaria

LEUCAS

ACARNANIA

Pindus Mts

A E G E A N   S E A

ITHACA

Missolonghi

Naupactus (Lepanto)

Parnassus △

Chaeronea

EUBOEA

JONIAN SEA

CEPHALONIA

Argostoli

Patras

Delphi

Lake Copais

Levadia

△Helicon

Thebes

CHIOS (SCIO)

ZANTE

Zante

PELOPONNESUS

Corinth

BOEOTIA

Eleusis

Kephissia

SALAMIS

ATHENS

ATTICA

Olympia

Nemea

Mycenae

Piraeus

ARCADIA

Nafplion

ÆGINA

Sunium

TENOS

Andritsaina

Bassae

POROS

Tenos

Kyparissia

Sparta

HYDRA

SYROS

Taygetus Mts

Mistras

Navarino

Naxos

NAXOS

0   50   100
Km

Miles

0   30   60

MELOS

SANTORINI Thera

80

A journey through Greece would start either from Corfu, for those who travelled through Germany or Northern Italy, or at Athens, for those who went by sea via Malta or Southern Italy. For a traveller who started from Corfu, it was convenient to begin the tour with the Ionian Islands – Paxos, Leucas, Cephalonia, Ithaca, Zante and Cythera – then cross to the coast of Epirus and visit Parga, Suli and Ioannina. From Ioannina the traveller could cross Thessaly and then continue northwards to Macedonia. To reach Athens, which was the centre of attraction on a Greek tour, the traveller could either proceed from Ioannina down the plains of Thessaly to Attica, or sail to the Gulf of Lepanto (Naupactus) and land at Patras. Landing at Patras, the traveller would either proceed through the northern Peloponnesus to Corinth, or would cross the Gulf of Lepanto to Missolonghi and pass Delphi, Mount Parnassus, Levadia and Thebes before arriving in Athens. Athens was of prime interest not only because of the attractions it provided in itself, but also because it was a convenient starting-point for tours of the rest of the country. For a tour of the Peloponnesus, the traveller could either go to Corinth, crossing the Isthmus and proceeding to Nafplion, or could take the boat to Nafplion, wander through the nearby ancient sites of Mycenae and Nemea, and then go south to Sparta and Mistras. From there, a long journey brought the traveller to Arcadia in central Morea, from where he could visit Bassae, Andritsaina and Olympia on the west coast of the peninsula, and then visit Corinth on the return journey to Athens. A cruise in the Aegean Islands would be undertaken by travellers who wished to go beyond this conventional itinerary. The islands of Salamis, Aegina, Poros and Hydra could all be visited from Athens in a day. The Cyclades – Tenos, Syros, Melos, Santorini – were not too far by boat from Piraeus, while the islands of the eastern Aegean – Chios, Rhodes – and Crete were mainly visited by those who were proceeding to the Near East.

The Ionian Islands

The Ionian Islands (Corfu, Paxos, Leucas, Cephalonia, Ithaca and Zante) extend in a chain opposite the coast of lower Albania, Epirus and Acarnania, while Cythera (Cerigo) is situated opposite the southern coast of the Peloponnesus. The islands were owned by the Venetians until 1797 when, by the Treaty of Campo Formio, they passed to the French. After a brief period of French occupation (1797–9), they were ruled by a Russo-Turkish condominium – an arrangement that ended as an exclusively Russian protectorate – until 1807, when they once more reverted to France. By 1814 the Ionian Islands were under British rule and, by the Treaty of Paris (November 1815), the 'United States of the Ionian Islands' came into being under British protection.

Corfu was the chief seat of government of the Septinsular Republic. In the nineteenth century it was the most popular of all the Ionian Islands with travellers, not only for the beauty of its scenery but also because it provided every comfort for the European visitor.

1 Joseph Cartwright, *The Town and Citadel of Corfu*, 1820

'The island is extremely picturesque. The west shore is an abrupt precipice, with exuberant foliage overhanging the sea. The south is closed by the Cheimerian promontory and the island of Leucadia . . . The north view is terminated by the steep and rocky Pantokrator . . . usually enveloped in clouds.'

Joseph Cartwright, *Views in the Ionian Islands*, 1821

The Citadel at Corfu was built by the Venetians in the mid-sixteenth century after the first siege of the city by the Turks in 1537; the upper part of the Citadel was added by the British in the nineteenth century.

2 John Frederick Lewis, *Distant View of the Citadel of Corfu*, 1840

'One of the greatest charms of Corfú [is] the perpetual framing of beautiful scenes by its twisted branches, and the veil-like glitter it throws around by its semi-transparent foliage. Everywhere the olive-tree grows in abundance and gracefulness . . . The whole island is in undulations from the plain where the city is, to the higher hills on the west side; all the space is covered with one immense grove of olive-trees, so that you see over a carpet of wood wherever you look; & the higher you go, the more you see and always the citadel & the lake and then the straits with the great Albanian mountains below.'

Edward Lear, letter to his sister Ann, Corfu, 19 June 1856

The island of Leucas is in fact a peninsula joined to the coast of Acarnania by a short isthmus. It was given the name Santa Maura by the Venetians. Cape Leucata, a rocky spur terminating in a high white cliff where the poetess Sappho is said to have been killed, is situated on the south-western coast of the island. Byron's 'Leucadia's far projecting rock of woe' was a favourite sight of nineteenth-century visitors.

'This grand cliff scene is at the South-western point of the Island of Santa Maura, and is well worthy of a visit, though not reached without considerable trouble. The great rocks rise boldly from the dark, deep waters, often raging against their base; and the solemn effect of that part which is in shadow is enhanced, in the early morning, by the bright light sparkling on the white crags, which, fringed by the wild cypress, overhang the gloomy depth below.

'On each of the two farthest cliffs are the remains of an ancient Temple – blocks of stone and scattered pottery; a spot once trodden by the feet of crowding votaries, now the haunt of the vulture and eagle.'

Edward Lear, *Views in the Seven Ionian Islands*, 1863

The island of Ithaca lies between the coast of Acarnania and Cephalonia, from which it is separated by a narrow channel.

'Ithaca, which owes its celebrity to the associated recollections of Ulysses, and to the divine poetry of Homer, is situated in the Ionian Sea . . . Ithaca still retains its ancient name among the upper class, though it is generally known by the appellation of Theaki . . . The population of the island amounts to about 8,000 persons, who inhabit Bathy the capital, and three small villages . . . Bathy is situated at the extremity of the port of the same name, which is deep and broad, and screened from the violence of the winds by the surrounding elevations . . . This is the port which is exhibited in the present view, and the lofty mountain beyond its entrance is the Neritos of Homer; but the soil is worn away, and the bare crags are no longer shaded by the waving forests which the poet has described.'

Edward Dodwell, *Views in Greece*, 1821

4 Edward Dodwell, *View of Ithaca*, 1801

Epirus, Thessaly and Macedonia

The traveller who wished to begin his Greek tour from northern Greece would cross from Corfu to the mainland and pursue his journey eastwards through the mountainous region of Epirus, then known as Albania. Following the road over the Pindus, he would reach the vast plain of Thessaly, which stretches to the Magnesian peninsula and is bordered on the east by Mounts Pelion, Ossa and Olympus. Passing through the valley of Tempe, between Olympus and Ossa, he would continue straight ahead and follow the road along the shore of the Thermaic Gulf to Salonica. From Salonica the traveller could visit the peninsula of Chalcidice and Mount Athos.

Parga, a small seaside town in Epirus, is opposite the island of Paxos. At the beginning of the nineteenth century it was a voivodeship, independent yet under the protection of Russia. Because of the threat of Ali Pasha of Ioannina, a French garrison was quartered there from 1807 to 1814, when the town was captured by the British. Five years later, when the British allowed Ali Pasha to take possession of the port of Parga, the town was destroyed and the entire population emigrated to Corfu.

5 Edward Lear, *View of Parga*, 1864

'About nine we arrived at beautiful and extensive groves of olive, for the cultivation of which Párga is renowned; they clothe all the hills around, and hang over rock and cliff to the very sea with delightful and feathery luxuriance . . . town and castle . . . at the foot of the little promontory . . . the islands in the bay, and the rich growth of olive slopes around, form a picture of completely beautiful character, though more resembling an Italian than a Greek scene . . .'

Edward Lear, *Journals of a Landscape Painter in Albania*, 1851

From Parga the traveller ascended the steep gorge of the Acheron to visit the celebrated village and fortress of Suli. In the eighteenth century Suli was still occupied by Christian Epirots who had been driven into the mountain regions by the invading Turks. From 1788 the Suliotes fought against Ali Pasha. In 1803 the remaining Suliotes, both men and women, instead of surrendering to Ali Pasha's victorious forces, either blew themselves and the enemy up with gunpowder or threw themselves from their mountain precipices. In Europe the Suliotes were compared with the ancient Spartans for their bravery during their long struggle against the Turks.

6 Edward Lear, *The Rocks of Suli*, 1849

'. . . the great rocks . . . of the "blood-stained Suli"! . . . For years those hills had rarely ceased to echo the cries of animosity, despair, and agony; now all is silent as the actors in that dreadful drama.

'Few scenes can compete in my memory with the wildness of this . . . and excepting in the deserts of the peninsula of Sinai, I have gazed on none more picturesque and strange.'

Edward Lear, *Journals of a Landscape Painter in Albania*, 1851

The Ionian Islands

VIII Joseph Schranz, *The Town and Citadel of Corfu from the Port*, c. 1840

'Corfú . . . lies so close to the lofty mountain-ranges of Epirus . . . as to include the grand features of the opposite coast in most of the views which can be taken from its own central hills. Whilst the noble line of the snowy Albanian heights thus forms the magnificent background of every picture if you look to the East, on the West the broad sea spreads from the foot of romantic precipices.'

Edward Lear, *Views in the Seven Ionian Islands*, 1863

IX Edward Lear, *View of the Town of Zante from the Castle Hill*, 1863

The island of Zante, called 'Fiore di Levante' by the Venetians, rivalled Corfu in its beautiful scenery, pleasant climate and social life. In the early nineteenth century the island was an important centre of cultural activity in the Ionian Islands.

'This is one of the most delightful scenes in Zante. The Town, with its gay white houses and its many tall and elegant campanili, spreads along the edge of the Bay beneath the Castle Hill, on the slopes of which, in beautiful contrast with them, thick groves of Olive, Orange, Cypress, and fruit-trees, cluster round the scattered villas. Beyond the Town, in the centre of the Drawing, is the mole, or quay; and on the other side of the Bay, where Village suburbs stretch away towards the plain, is the high belfry of Saint Dionysius, the Patron Saint of the Island. The hill opposite is Mount Skopó, about 1500 feet in height. Its form is peculiarly graceful, and its sides are furrowed by hollows which, up to a considerable height, are covered with corn and groves of olives. 'In the distance are seen the hills of the Morea, and in the foreground Olives and Aloes; the latter being very abundant on the rocks and by the way-sides in Zante.'

Edward Lear, *Views in the Seven Ionian Islands*, 1863

X Edward Lear, *View of Argostoli in Cephalonia*, 1864

Cephalonia, the largest island in the Ionian Sea, lies eight miles north of Zante, opposite the coast of Acarnania and the entrance to the Gulf of Corinth.

'Argostolí is the Capital of Cephalonia, and is built on a rising ground at the head of the Harbour on its western side. A long causeway divides the Port from the shallow water at its southern end; and a fine carriage road . . . winds to the great pine-forest at the top of the Black Mountain . . . immediately over the City. . . . The buildings of Argostolí are handsome, and the town, though not remarkable for liveliness, possesses many good streets and public edifices. The foreground is a path of gray rocks, where the lentisk grows and the broad-leaved squill abounds, and thence groves of olives cover the slopes to the city below.'

Edward Lear, *Views in the Seven Ionian Islands*, 1863

VIII

Squills
not possible to draw
for flies. I being obliged
to sit in the sunshine.

Zante. 26. May. 1863. 2 & 3.40. P.M.

(201)

IX

X

XI

XII

XIV

Epirus, Thessaly and Macedonia

XI William Gell, *The Valley of Tempe*, 1805

After journeying for several days through the dusty plains of Thessaly (pls 12–13), the traveller would be relieved to reach the shady valley of Tempe, a narrow pass between Mounts Ossa and Olympus that provided the only accessible route to Macedonia.

'. . . this most celebrated "vale" . . . is a narrow pass – and although extremely beautiful, on account of the precipitous rocks on each side, the Peneus flowing deep in the midst, between the richest overhanging plane woods, still its character is distinctly that of a ravine or gorge. . . . Well might the ancients extol this grand defile, where the landscape is so completely different from that of any part of Thessaly, and awakes the most vivid feelings of awe and delight, from its associations with the legendary history and religious rites of Greece.'

Edward Lear, *Journals of a Landscape Painter in Albania*, 1851

XII Edward Lear, *The Monastery of Dionysiou, Mount Athos*, 1862

The monastery of Dionysiou was founded in 1370–74 by St Dionysius of Korseos and was later financially supported by Alexius III, Emperor of Trebizond. In the nineteenth century there were twenty monasteries altogether on the peninsula of Haghion Oros (The Holy Mountain). (See also pl. 15)

The road to Athens

XIII Edward Lear, *View of Mount Parnassus and the Plains of Boeotia*, 1862

Ascending from Delphi (pls 19–21), the traveller reached Mount Parnassus, sacred home of Apollo and the Muses. Its summit offered the most striking panoramic views of the Gulf of Corinth and the mountains of the Peloponnesus to the south, Mount Olympus to the north, and the many ridges of Mount Pindus to the east.

'Oh, thou Parnassus! whom I now survey,
Not in the phrenzy of a dreamer's eye,
Not in the fabled landscape of a lay,
But soaring snow-clad through thy native sky,
In the wild pomp of mountain majesty!

Byron, *Childe Harold's Pilgrimage*, 1812

XIV Karl Rottmann, *The Plain of Chaeronea and Lake Copais*, 1835

From Levadia (pl. 22), the traveller could easily make the excursion northwards to Lake Copais and Chaeronea, site of the famous battle in which Philip of Macedonia decisively defeated a coalition of the Greek cities in 338 BC.

'The lake which was formerly called the Cephissian or Copaic, [is] . . . now the lake of Topolias. In this plain is the city of Chaeronea; it stands on . . . the north side of a rocky hill . . . Below it is the field on which was fought the celebrated battle which laid the city of Athens at the feet of Philip of Macedon, – on which was won
" – that dishonest victory . . . fatal to liberty, whose tidings killed that old man eloquent."'

Christopher Wordsworth, *Greece: Pictorial, Descriptive and Historical*, 1839

Any traveller to Epirus in the early nineteenth century would not have omitted to visit Ioannina, the seat of Ali Pasha. Ali was nominally a vassal of the Sultan, but through military skill and intrigue had risen to be ruler of Epirus and the whole south-western part of the Balkan peninsula. Byron, who visited Ioannina in 1809, was very impressed when he was entertained in the Pasha's palace.

'The situation of Ioannina, the capital of Ali, is magnificent. Resting on a gentle descent, it extends along a narrow promontory, which projects far into the lake, whose waters are darkened with the shade of impending mountains, amongst which the range of Pindus is visible . . . the effect of the whole scene is striking and picturesque; the broad dome of the mosques, the slender column of the minarets, the lofty cypresses, and the range of the Vizir's palaces . . . afford most interesting subjects for the pencil . . . In the scanty list of modern Greek authors, the natives of Ioannina hold a conspicuous situation. In the barbarous districts of Epirus, we must now seek for the glimmering of that light which once illuminated the territory of Attica.'

William Haygarth, *Greece, a Poem*, 1814

7 William Haygarth, *View of Ioannina*, 1810

'I descended to the lake; there, on the small island which rises from its southern part, I discovered a pretty village where I counted seven monasteries. Almost opposite, a sort of promontory extends, which is dominated by the fortress and the old seraglio, and which forms the eastern extremity of Mount Paktoros, separated from the city by a navigable channel. On all sides my eyes rested in delight: at times I followed the fishing boats, at times the wild birds whose movement and rapid flight animated the whole scene; I found it difficult to emerge from the delightful sensations in which I had been plunged in order to draw the view of the seraglio and the fortress.'

Louis Dupré, *Voyage à Athènes et Constantinople*, 1825

8 William Page, *The Lake of Ioannina*, c. 1820

Because of the prosperity of its inhabitants, the city of Ioannina became one of the most significant centres of intellectual activity in Greece in the early nineteenth century. Similar developments occurred in other parts of Greece at this time and gave rise to the intellectual revival that constituted the background to the movement for Greek independence.

'The house . . . of Signore Nicolo Argyri . . . is the same which Lord Byron and Mr Hobhouse occupied during their residence in Ioannina, and . . . it affords perhaps as good a specimen as can be met with of a modern Greek mansion . . . From the street we enter by a pair of folding doors . . . into a large stone portico or piazza, enclosing three sides of an area or court fronted by a garden, which is separated from it by a palisade: in the basement story, which is flanked by this portico, are stables, granaries, and other offices: very near the folding doors a flight of stone steps lead up to a fine picturesque gallery or corridor . . . supported on the stone arches of the portico and shaded by the long shelving roof of the house; this is a place of exercise for the inmates in bad weather, and of indolent repose during the violence of the heat: at one end is seen a species of summer-house fitted up with seats and cushions, called the kiosk, where the family sit to enjoy the refreshing breeze, and the master frequently receives his visitors; at the other end is a bath. From the gallery we enter at once into the dwelling rooms, the principal of which are the apartments of the men . . . At a different part of the gallery a passage leads into the gynaeconitis or gynaecéum . . . the apartments of the women, which are in general smaller than those of the men, and are for the most part entered through a small anteroom or passage.'

The Rev. Thomas Smart Hughes, *Travels in Sicily, Greece and Albania*, 1820

9 Charles Robert Cockerell, *A Greek House in Ioannina*, 1811

From Ioannina, the traveller could visit the spectacular mountain site of Meteora in northern Thessaly, with its monasteries dating from the fourteenth century AD. *Widespread brigandage and wars had caused many monasteries in Greece to be built in remote and inaccessible locations.*

10 Edward Lear, *View of Meteora,* 1848/63

'I do not think I ever saw any scene so startling and incredible; such vast sheer perpendicular pyramids, standing out of the earth, with the tiny houses of the village clustering at the roots. . . . Strange, unearthly-looking rocks are these, full of gigantic chasms and round holes, resembling Gruyère cheese, as it were, highly magnified, their surface being otherwise perfectly smooth. . . . The magnificent foreground of fine oak and detached fragments of rock, struck me as one of the peculiar features of the scene. The detached and massive pillars of stone, crowned with the retreats of the monks, rise perpendicularly from the sea of foliage, which . . . is wrapped in the deepest shade, while the bright eastern light strikes the upper part of the magic heights with brilliant force and breadth. To make any real use of the most exquisite landscape abounding throughout this marvellous spot, an artist should stay here for a month. . .'

Edward Lear, *Journals of a Landscape Painter in Albania,* 1851

11 Otto Magnus von Stackelberg, *The Monastery of Varlaam at Meteora*, 1812

'The Greek monasteries of Meteora are variously situated, either on the summits of these pinnacles, or in caverns, which nature and art have united to form in parts of the rock, that seem inapproachable by the foot of man. . . . The only access to these aerial prisons is by ropes, or by ladders fixed firmly to the rock, in those places where its surface affords any points of suspension; and these ladders, in some instances connected with artificial subterranean tunnels, which give a passage of easier access to the buildings above. . . .

'The number of monasteries at Meteora is said to have been formerly twenty-four; but at present, owing partly to the wearing away of the rocks on which they stood, partly to the decay of the buildings themselves, only ten of these remain: – Meteora or Meteoron, Aios Stephanos, Barlaam, Aia Triada, Aios Nicholas, Rosaria, and Aia Mono . . . the monastery of Barlaam appears to have been founded in 1536, by Nectarius of Ioannina, and another Greek called Theophanes . . .'

Henry Holland, *Travels in the Ionian Isles, Albania, Thessaly, Macedonia, &c.*, 1815

Larissa was one of the principal commercial centres of Thessaly. Travellers were often surprised to discover that caravans departed regularly from the town to Macedonia and beyond.

'At the base of this vaste barrier of mountains is situated the town of LARISSA, extending in a long line, and making a magnificent appearance. . . . The town is situated upon the PENEUS, now called *Salambrîa*; and there is a very handsome bridge over the river, the buttresses being lightened by perforations: it consists of sixteen arches . . . From this river the inhabitants are well supplied with fish . . . Here we saw . . . in use, those antique cars, drawn by oxen or by buffaloes, with solid wheels . . .'

Edward Daniel Clarke, *Travels in Various Countries of Europe, Asia and Africa*, 1810–23

Mount Pelion, in the Magnesian peninsula, formed the eastern boundary of the plain of Thessaly. Besides being a favourite spot with travellers because of its remarkable beauty, it was also exceptionally rich in mythological associations. It was here, for instance, that the centaur Chiron, the tutor of Jason and Achilles, lived.

'Mount Pelion is adorned with about twenty-four large and opulent villages, or rather towns, most of which are inhabited by Greeks of hardy habits and athletic forms. Portaria which is one of the most considerable . . . is situated high up the southern acclivity of the mountain, in the midst of a varied profusion of trees, which form cooling arbours and embowering shades, while the streets are irrigated by numerous streams that ripple under the luxuriant canopy of wide-spreading platani, and amid the chequered decorations of the clustering vine. The scenery is rich in distant prospect, and in every variety of immediate embellishment. Nature here seems to assume her most captivating attire, and to revel in her most fantastic forms. Here is delight for the voluptuous, incitement for the romantic, and repose for the weary. No locality can well interest the imagination or gratify the sight by a greater profusion of charms. The associations of old times are diffused around; and plenty, with a sort of spontaneous promptitude, seems to start up from the bosom of the teeming soil without the aid of elaborate cultivation. . . .

'The poetical fancy of the ancient Greeks has left the majestic elevation of Pelion surrounded with a never-fading glory of mythological wonders and classic charms. The mighty forms of giants and centaurs still flit over the sacred soil wherever it is beheld by a mind that has been touched by the transport of the classic page. He who has once experienced the potent illusion, which this fascinating scenery is calculated to excite, will not readily disengage his mind from the magic of the view.'

Edward Dodwell, *Views in Greece*, 1821

13 Simone Pomardi, *The Village of Portaria on Mount Pelion*, 1806

14 Edward Lear, *View of Salonica (Thessaloniki) and the Thermaic Gulf,* 1848

Following the road northwards from Larissa along the shore, the traveller would reach the Macedonian town of Salonica at the head of the Thermaic Gulf. Lear's view is taken from the Vlatadon Monastery in the Upper Town on the northern side of the city.

'From the convent at the summit of the town, just within its white walls, the view . . . [is] most glorious . . . I saw an infinity of picturesque bits . . . the silvery minarets relieving the monotonous surface of roofs below . . . the delicately indented shore and blue gulf . . . and all the range of Olympus.'

Edward Lear, *Journals of a Landscape Painter in Albania,* 1851

Mount Athos, situated in the easternmost peninsula of Chalcidice, was difficult to reach; but its wild and romantic scenery, and its monasteries – the oldest dating from the tenth century AD *– provided the traveller with an unforgettable experience.*

'Tὸ Ἅγιον Ὄρος or the Holy Mountain, [is] altogether the most surprising thing I have seen in my travels, perhaps, barring Egypt. It is a pensinsular mountain about 2000 ft. high & 50 miles long ending in a vast crag, near 7000 feet high, this being Athos. All but this bare crag is one mass of vast forest, beech, chestnut, oak & ilex, and all round the cliffs and crags by the sea are 20 great and ancient monistirries . . . These convents are inhabited by, altogether perhaps, 6 or 7000 monx, & as you may have heard, no female creature exists in all the peninsula: – there are nothing but mules, tomcats, & cocks allowed. This is literally true.'

Edward Lear, letter to Chichester Fortescue, Corfu, 9 October 1856

'On the Holy Mountain, as elsewhere, the founders of monasteries have usually shown great taste in the selection of their sites . . . *Kutlumush* . . . is . . . in the most cultivable part of the peninsula, among gardens, vineyards, olive plantations and cornfields. This is the smallest of all the convents, not containing above 30 caloyers. It was founded during the reign of Andronicus the Elder (AD 1283–1328) by Constantine, a noble of the Turkish family of Kutlumush, related to the Seljuk Sultans. His mother was a Christian, and on her death he embraced Christianity, and became a monk of Mount Athos.'

John Murray, *A Handbook for Travellers in Greece*, 1854

15 Edward Lear, *The Monastery of Koutloumoussiou, Mount Athos*, 1856

The road to Athens

Patras was the first point on the Peloponnesus at which the boat journeying through the Ionian Islands would touch. This was one of the busiest ports in Greece, facilitating communication by sea with the adjacent islands and the Adriatic Sea. To reach Athens from Patras by the mainland, the traveller would then cross the narrow channel that forms the entrance to the Gulf of Lepanto and land at Missolonghi. From there the road wound its way along the coast, then crossed the plain of Crissa to Kastri, from where a steep ascent brought the traveller to the summit of Mount Parnassus. Continuing towards Boeotia, Mount Helicon and the town of Levadia could be seen in the distance. From Levadia, a short detour could easily be made to visit Chaeronea before continuing southwards to Thebes, Eleusis and, finally, Athens.

16 Hugh William Williams, *A Street in Patras*, 1817

'Patras, the ancient Patrae, now a town of considerable size, stands upon a rising ground of gentle elevation . . . The mountains behind . . . are lofty, of noble and pleasing forms, especially the snow-capped Vodia . . . The streets of Patras are very narrow . . . The roofs of the houses almost meet, which, no doubt, is intended for shade in this warm climate.'

Hugh William Williams, *Travels in Italy, Greece and the Ionian Islands*, 1820

Missolonghi is situated near the entrance of the Gulf of Patras on the north coast. The town is a landmark in the history of the War of Independence because of the exceptional courage of its people when they were besieged by the Turks in 1825–6. Byron and Hobhouse spent three days there in November 1809. In January 1824 Byron went there again and was settled in the house which he shared with Colonel Stanhope, an agent of the London Philhellenic Committee. After Byron's death from fever at Missolonghi in April 1824, the town rapidly became a place of pilgrimage for all Philhellenes.

17 William Purser, *View of Missolonghi with Lord Byron's House, 1824*

18 Edward Dodwell, *Dinner in a Greek House at Crissa*, 1801

'The large village of Crisso, which probably occupies the site of the ancient Krissa, is situated in the ancient territory of Phocis on the southern side of Parnassos, and about six miles west of the ruins of Delphi. The Bishop of Salona, who resides at this place, gave us reception in his house. We dined in an open gallery which commanded a magnificent view over the shores of the Crissaean Gulf.

'Before sitting down to dinner . . . we performed the ancient ceremony of washing the hands. A tin bason is taken round to all the company, the servant holding it on his left arm, while with his right hand he pours water from a pewter vessel on the hands of the washer, having a towel thrown over his shoulder to dry them with. This ceremony . . . is mentioned by Hesiod, by Homer, and other authors.

'We dined at a round table supported on one leg or column, like the *monopodia* of the ancients. We sat on cushions placed on the floor. The dish in the middle of the table is *pilau*, composed of rice and boiled meat. The circular cakes, which are a fine kind of bread, are named *colouri*.

'The venerable figure reclining on the left hand is the Bishop of Salona. This prelate is receiving the hommage of a Greek peasant, who kisses the ground before he applies his lips to the bishop's hand. The man holding the water-bason is an Albanian christian, and the person washing is a Greek gentleman. The middle figure at the table is a village priest designated by the black cap. The woman bringing in a fowl, is an Albanian.'

Edward Dodwell, *Views in Greece*, 1821

110

Following the shore of the northern coast of the Gulf of Lepanto the traveller would cross the Crissaean plain to reach Delphi. However, with the exception of the majestic scenery – which was in itself evocative of a holy place – very little was to be seen at the celebrated site of the Sanctuary of Apollo, for, until the end of the nineteenth century, Delphi was overlaid by the village of Kastri.

'Oh, thou! in Hellas deem'd of heavenly birth,
Muse! form'd or fabled at the minstrel's will!
Since shamed full oft by later lyres on earth,
Mine dares not call thee from thy sacred hill:
Yet there I've wander'd by thy vaunted rill;
Yes! sigh'd o'er Delphi's long-deserted shrine,
Where, save that feeble fountain, all is still . . .

'Though here no more Apollo haunts his grot,
And thou, the Muses' seat, art now their grave,
Some gentle spirit still pervades the spot,
Sighs in the gale, keeps silence in the cave,
And glides with glassy foot o'er yon melodious wave.'

Byron, *Childe Harold's Pilgrimage*, 1812

19 Edward Lear, *View of the
Village of Kastri, Delphi*, 1849–50

20 André Louis de Sinety, *The Castalian Spring at Delphi*, 1847

21 John Fulleylove, *Stoa of the Athenians at Delphi*, 1895

The Stoa of the Athenians is situated on the left of the Sacred Way of the Temenos at Delphi, against the retaining wall of the Temple of Apollo. The work of excavation at Delphi was begun in 1838 but could only be completed after the expropriation of the village of Kastri in 1891.

'The wall of polygonal masonry to the right is part of the . . . terrace wall, of the Great Temple of Apollo. Three marble steps at the back of the Athenian portico, with two Ionic columns in place, stand in front of the wall. The sacred way, terminating at the east end of the Great Temple above, passes in front of the portico . . . To the left of the drawing is seen the mountain slope of Kirphis leading down to the gorge of the river Pleistos.'

John Fulleylove, *Greece,* 1906

'A short distance from Kastri the rock actually splits in two to form a kind of cavern open to the sky and difficult of access: it was here that the Priestess of Apollo used to sit. To the right there is a little spring whose water is channelled into a shallow pool which can be reached by the three or four remaining steps. This was the Castalian Spring where the Priestess used to bathe before taking her seat at the Oracle. In front of the spring there were once several buildings, traces of which can be seen on the rock. The water from the spring is sweet and fresh.'

Antoine de Latour, *Voyage de S.A.R. Monseigneur le duc de Montpensier à Tunis, en Egypte, en Turquie et en Grèce,* 1847

22 William Walker, *View of Levadia*, 1803

Ascending the north-east slopes of Mount Helicon, the traveller reached Levadia, the only other town in Boeotia comparable in importance with Thebes. But whereas in the nineteenth century Thebes was a poverty-stricken village, Levadia was a prosperous town set in idyllic scenery. In classical times Levadia was the site of the oracle of Trophonios – second in repute only to that of Delphi itself.

'The town of Livadhía has an imposing appearance from the northward, and forms a scene no less singular than beautiful. Its houses are surrounded for the most part with gardens, and thus occupy a large space of ground on some steep acclivities at the foot of a precipitous height which is crowned with a ruined castle, said to have been built by the Catalans. This height is an abrupt northerly termination of Mount *Helicon*, and is separated eastward from similar hills by a torrent issuing from the mountain between lofty precipices, and falling with great rapidity over a rocky bed as it passes through the middle of the town. . . . There are springs also in many parts of the site; so that by the effect of this abundance of water, combined with the shelter of the overhanging mountains, the air in the summer, in the upper part of the town, during an hour or two in the morning and evening, has a most agreeable coolness . . .'

Colonel William Martin Leake, *Travels in Northern Greece*, 1835

OVERLEAF

Following the road from Levadia to the south-east, the traveller came to an extensive plain, in the midst of which, on an eminence, rose the town of Thebes.

'From a hilltop named Cadmeia, on the other side of Thebes, the rivulet of Ismenos can be seen in the foreground, bordered by lentisk bushes and shaded by a line of trees with dense foliage . . . The modern city occupies the site of Cadmeia, the ancient fortified city of Cadmus, which proves how big a city it originally was. At the very edge of the city is a high tower, which was built on the site of one of the seven ancient Gates. On the left of the view is an aqueduct upon a series of arches that carries the water to the highest point of the new city, and which is surrounded by many cypresses and plane-trees.'

Otto Magnus von Stackelberg, *La Grèce. Vues pittoresques et topographiques*, 1834

23 Hugh William Williams, *View of Thebes*, 1819

24 Théodore du Moncel, *View of Eleusis, c. 1843*

The road from Eleusis to Athens followed the route of the ancient Sacred Way along which the annual procession to the Sanctuary of Demeter used to pass from Athens.

'The road from Athens to Eleusis is built partly on the ancient sacred road . . . At its end, the actual village of Eleusis appears as if by enchantment, and one sees the sea and Lake Rheti, both of which in antiquity were consecrated to Demeter and Persephone . . . Nowadays the latter is a muddy swamp where lentisk bushes and reeds grow in confusion . . . The ancient acropolis is situated on the mountain . . . The Venetian tower that can be seen on the hill on the right rests upon ancient foundations . . . I visited some of the houses of this poor village; they are just miserable huts, most of them built of earth and with one storey.'

Théodore du Moncel, *De Venise à Constantinople à travers la Grèce, c. 1843*

Athens

'The specific quality of Athenian landscape is light – not richness or sublimity or romantic loveliness or grandeur of mountain outline, but luminous beauty, serene exposure to the airs of heaven . . . Ἰοστέφανος is an epithet of Aristophanes for his city; and if not crowned with other violets, Athens wears for her garland the air-empurpled hills – Hymettus, Lycabettus, Pentelicus, and Parnes . . . From whatever point the plain of Athens . . . may be surveyed, it always presents a picture of dignified and lustrous beauty. The Acropolis is the centre of this landscape, splendid as a work of art with its own crown of temples.

'. . . Athens, like the Greeks of history, is isolated in a sort of self-completion: she is a thing of the past, which still exists, because the spirit never dies, because beauty is a joy for ever. What is truly remarkable about the city is just this, that while the modern town is an insignificant mushroom of the present century, the monuments of Greek art in the best period – the masterpieces of Ictinus and Mnesicles, and the theatre on which the plays of the tragedians were produced – survive in comparative perfection, and are so far unencumbered with subsequent edifices that the actual Athens of Pericles absorbs our attention.'

John Addington Symonds, *Sketches and Studies in Italy and Greece*, 1898

25 Raffaello Ceccoli, *View of the Acropolis with the Theatre of Herodes Atticus, c.* 1850

Coming from the Eleusis road, through the groves of Plato's Academy, the traveller gained his first view of Athens, with the precipitous rock of the Acropolis rising in the middle and the hill of Lycabettus on the left, set against the impressive mass of Mount Hymettus.

'The view of Athens from the road to Eleusis . . . [gives] perhaps the most beautiful as well as the most explanatory idea of the position of the Acropolis with reference to the country by which it is surrounded . . . To the left of the drawing is the Lycabettus . . . while the mountain forming a common background to this, as well as other portions of the landscape, is the far-famed, bee-thronged Hymettus . . . With a profound contempt for all the common-place conventionality by which so many feel compelled to go into raptures upon certain occasions, and with the strongest feeling of the propriety of controlling these as well as other emotions, I confess that I should have but little respect for any educated man, who could find himself within a few miles of the city of Minerva, and retain at all his normal mental condition.'

Henry Cook, *Recollections of a Tour in the Ionian Islands, Greece and Constantinople*, 1853

26 Henry Cook, *View of Athens from the Road to Eleusis*, 1850

The Acropolis remained in the possession of the Turks until the spring of 1833, when a small Bavarian garrison was installed in the name of the Greek state. From the summer of 1831 onwards, the Acropolis ceased to be used as a fortress, and it was declared an archaeological site.

27 William Page, *View of the Acropolis, c. 1820*

'How can I, by description, give you any idea of the great pleasure I enjoyed in the sight of these ancient buildings of Athens! How strongly were exemplified in them the grandeur and effect of simplicity in architecture!'

Robert Smirke, diary, 1803

28 Hugh William Williams, *The Parthenon*, 1819

'. . . in viewing the Parthenon, we were so much affected by its solemn appearance, and so much dazzled by its general splendor and magnificence, that we should never have ventured to . . . [any] critical examination of the parts composing it . . . Often as it has been described, the spectator who for the first time approaches it finds that nothing he has read can give any idea of the effect produced in beholding it. Yet was there once found in England a writer of eminence in his profession as an architect, who recommended the study of Roman antiquities in Italy and in France, in preference to the remains of Grecian architecture in Athens; and who, deciding upon the works of Phidias, Callicrates, and Ictinus, without ever having had an opportunity to examine them but in books and prints, ventured to maintain that the Parthenon was not so considerable an edifice as the Church of St. Martin in London; thereby affording a remarkable proof of the impossibility of obtaining from any written description, or even from engraved representation, any adequate idea of the buildings of Antient Greece; compared with whose stupendous works, the puny efforts of modern art are but as the labours of children.'

Edward Daniel Clarke, *Travels in Various Countries of Europe, Asia and Africa*, 1810–23

Under the Turks, the Erechtheum was used as the harem of the governor of Athens.

'The Temple of Minerva Polias, or, as it is sometimes called, the Erectheum, is of Ionic architecture, nor has there ever existed a more perfect specimen of that graceful order. In length it is seventy-three feet, and in breadth thirty-seven, measuring the interior cella, without counting the portico of six pillars at the eastern end. Another portico of four pillars in front, with two retiring pillars, adorned the northern side of the building. At the opposite side is the beautiful porch of the Caryatides, in which Virgins attired in the religious costume of the Panathenaic solemnity take the place of pillars, and support the projecting cornice on their broad and sedate brows, which in that cornice seem rather to wear a crown than to sustain a burthen.'

Aubrey De Vere, *Picturesque Sketches of Greece and Turkey,* 1850

29 Hugh William Williams, *View of the Erechtheum,* 1819

30 Ippolito Caffi, *The Propylaea*, 1843

31 Ippolito Caffi, *Interior of the Parthenon*, 1843

32 Ippolito Caffi, *The Parthenon and the Erechtheum*, 1843

'We see Athens in ruins. On the central rock of its ACROPOLIS, exist the remains in a mutilated state, of three temples – the Temple of VICTORY, the PARTHENON, and the ERECTHEUM. Of the PROPYLAEA . . . some walls and a few columns are still standing. Of the THEATRE on the south side of the Acropolis, in which the dramas of Aeschylus, Sophocles, and Euripides were represented, some stone steps remain . . . But . . . while we are forcibly and mournfully reminded by this spectacle, of the perishable nature of the most beautiful objects which the world has seen . . . we are naturally led by it to contrast the permanence and vitality of the *spirit* and *intelligence* which produced these works . . . Not at Athens alone are we to look for Athens. The epitaph, – *Here is the heart: the spirit is every where*, – may be applied to it . . . These buildings now before us, ruined as they are at present, have served for two thousand years as models for the most admired fabrics in every civilized country of the world . . . Thus the genius which conceived and executed these magnificent works, while the materials on which it laboured are dissolved, has itself proved immortal.'

Christopher Wordsworth, *Greece: Pictorial, Descriptive and Historical*, 1839

125

The Temple of Apteros Nike, or Athena Nike, was built in 427–424 BC from designs by Callicrates. It stood at the foot of the Propylaea until 1687, when it was destroyed by the Turks to make way for a bastion. It was restored in 1835–9.

33 J. N. H. de Chacaton, *The Temple of Apteros Nike (Wingless Victory)*, 1839

'The Temple of Victory without Wings is, with the exception of the pavement, entirely a restoration; for nearly two centuries all trace of it was lost, all mention omitted. In renovating one of the Turkish batteries, in order to clear an entrance to the Propylaea, some fragments were found which led to a minute investigation; and, after a short time, the foundation, the pavement, and even the bases of some of the columns were disinterred, making its re-construction not only very easy, but extremely satisfactory. It is small, but of exquisite proportions, and now perfect, with the exception of a portion of the frieze, which is in the British Museum.'

Henry Cook, 'The Present State of the Monuments of Greece', 1851

'The beauty of the temples I well knew from endless drawings – but the immense sweep of plain with exquisitely formed mountains down to the sea – & the manner that huge mass of rock – the Acropolis – stands above the modern town with its glittering white marble ruins against the deep blue sky is quite beyond my expectations . . . poor old scrubby Rome sinks into nothing by the side of such beautiful magnificence.'

Edward Lear, letter to his sister Ann, Athens, 3 June 1848

34 Carl Haag, *View of the Acropolis*, 1861

XV Johann Jacob Wolfensberger, *View of Athens from the Ilissus,* 1834

On leaving the Olympieum (pl. 37), the visitor reached the River Ilissus which ran from its source on the northern slopes of Mount Hymettus down in a gentle arc between Lycabettus and the Hill of Ardettus where the Stadium stood. Although in the nineteenth century the river was almost completely dried up, the location was nonetheless rich in classical associations: it was the verdant banks of the Ilissus that inspired Socrates' lyrical description at the beginning of Plato's Phaedrus.

'We sat down in the Temple of the Muses, on the west bank of the river . . . nearly opposite the Stadium . . . How delightful was the view that surrounded us! To the North-West was Athens, with the Acropolis and all its prominent antiquities, except the Temple of Theseus, which we could not see, as it was on the other side. Near that part of the city . . . built at the bottom of the hill, was an olive grove . . . To the west of us was the Piraeus and the glorious Salamis. To the east rose the long ridge of Hymettus, and to the north Mount Anchesmus (with a smaller mountain to the left of it) . . . and on the plain below stood another large olive grove on the banks of the Ilissus.'

William Turner, *Journal of a Tour in the Levant,* 1820

XVI Hugh William Williams, *View of the Propylaea,* 1819

The Propylaea, which in the thirteenth century had been transformed into the palace of the Florentine Dukes Acciaiuoli, was cleared in 1836–7, and the Pinakotheke in its north wing was used as a museum. In 1884 all the antiquities were transferred to the Acropolis Museum.

'The scene of desolation in the Acropolis is complete . . . heaps of ruins of wretched houses and various buildings, constructed part with clay and marble, the marble looking doleful through the mud . . . I went . . . to the top of the ancient Propyleà, which, certainly, presents the finest view of the whole of the Acropolis, and, perhaps, is yet matchless in the world. In front appears the Temple of Minerva, augustly beautiful, the sunbeams stealing among the lovely columns, and casting shadows in the deep recess . . . and the pillars of the Propyleà shoot through the crumbling ruins of successive ages . . . Often in the course of my travels I have felt the force of a sentiment which I have somewhere seen expressed, that every thing sublime and noble is more or less allied to emotions of melancholy. With such a scene before me as that which I now contemplate, the pulse goes quicker, and the tears fill the eye, but not with those of delight.'

Hugh William Williams, *Travels in Italy, Greece and the Ionian Islands,* 1820

XVII Jean Baptiste Hilaire, *A Marriage in Athens, c.* 1800

In the nineteenth century Greek weddings were marked by a good deal of ceremonial. The wedding procession would be preceded by dancers and musicians; then followed the bridegroom on horseback accompanied by his friends; last of all came the bride, decorated in all her jewellery and covered in a long veil, surrounded by her girl-friends.

XV

XVI

XVII

XVIII

XIX

XX

XXI

XXII

XVIII   Théodore Aligny, *Greek Girls Dancing the 'Romaika'*, 1850

Athenians were renowned for their gaity and love of festivities. The visitor was thus often presented with the opportunity of enjoying the spectacle of the Greek national dance which was called the 'Romaika'.

XIX   Charles Lock Eastlake, *The Erechtheum*, 1820

Eastlake recorded in his journal: 'Admittance to the Acropolis was purchased by a present of three or four dollars to the Disdar Aga . . . We drew there in perfect tranquillity . . . From the day I first sat down to draw . . . the only journal I kept was not in black and white, but in blue, red and yellow.'

XX   J. N. H. de Chacaton, *Hadrian's Library*, 1839

Hadrian's Library was known variously as the Stoa Poikile, Pantheon, or Gymnasium of Hadrian, before its identity was established by the excavations in 1885. Against it stood the Byzantine Church of the Taxiarchs, or Megali Panaghia, that was demolished at the time of the excavations.

'The Stoa of Adrian, standing in the present market-place, is nearly hidden by surrounding buildings; a ruined church conceals several of the columns, the Corinthian capitals of which appear above the roof; the others are exposed, and each of one block of marble: there are seven of these, with another, which stands out alone, fluted.'

Edward Giffard, *A Short Visit to the Ionian Islands, Athens, and the Morea*, 1838

XXI   Vicenzo Lanza, *View of the Area around the Theseum*, 1869

Built between 449 and 444 BC on a hill overlooking the Agora, the Theseum was the best preserved of all Greek temples. It owed its name to the fact that its frieze was decorated with scenes from the life of Theseus, although it was originally consecrated to Hephaestus. From the sixth century onwards it was used as the Christian Church of St George. In 1835 it became the first archaeological museum in Athens.

'After the war of independence, Athens was little more than a heap of ruins with unroofed houses and deserted streets . . . At the present time, 1869, Athens is a well-built and rapidly increasing town, with about seventy thousand inhabitants. . . . The temple of Theseus . . . stands on an isolated hill, round which the modern carriage road, from the Acropolis to the railway station, sweeps . . . It now serves as a museum, in which are stored altars, statues, and other remains of art, in a more or less mutilated condition.'

Frederick Trench Townshend, *A Cruise in Greek Waters*, 1870

XXII   James Skene, *View of Kephissia*, 1839

By the middle of the nineteenth century the village of Kephissia, to the north-east of Athens, had become a popular country resort for Athenians.

'. . . Kifisía . . . [is] vulgarly pronounced Kifishá or Tjifishá. Here are several large pyrghi with good gardens, and a mosque, before which are a fountain and a beautiful plane-tree. The rare advantage in *Attica* of an abundance of running water in the middle of summer has rendered this place a favourite abode of the Turks of Athens . . .'

Colonel William Martin Leake, *Travels in Northern Greece*, 1835

35 Ferdinand Stademann, *A
Panoramic View of Athens*, 1835

'Athens, formerly the capital of Attica, and nowadays the capital of the
Kingdom of Greece, is situated . . . in a plain which is often interrupted by
hills, and bounded on the east by Mount Vrellissos or Pentelicon, on the south
by Hymettus, on the west by Korydallos and the Saronic Gulf, whose waves
water the ports of Piraeus and Mounychia and Phaleron, and on the north by
Mount Aegaleos. We see here a picture composed of buildings dating from
various periods, very much distant one from the other.'

Ferdinand Stademann, *Panorama von Athen*, 1841

The Parthenon was consecrated during the Crusades as the Church of St Mary the Virgin of Athens. It was transformed into a mosque in 1460. After the Liberation, the mosque was used as a museum until it was demolished in 1842.

'However long we might linger among the ruins of this most majestic and beautiful of temples, I should expect you to pronounce our stay far too brief, and should be much disappointed if you did not declare that no description has yet done justice to its grandeur and beauty. In any anathema you might utter against the builders of the unsightly structure, by turns mosque and church, which cumbers the precinct of the holy of holies, I should most heartily sympathize; and not less so in any tribute of admiration, however extravagant, you might be disposed to offer to the lordly citizen in whose brain the beauteous fabric first was reared.'

Edgar Garston, *Greece Revisited*, 1842

36 Karl Wilhelm von Heydeck,
*View of the Parthenon with the
Church of the Virgin*, 1834

37 Thomas Hartley Cromek, *The Olympieum*, 1844

The Temple of Olympian Zeus, to the east of the Acropolis, was begun in the late sixth century BC and finally completed by the Emperor Hadrian in AD 131–2. With its gigantic columns rising perpendicularly in the midst of a vast platform, it appeared to the nineteenth-century visitor as a model of the sublimity of classical Greek art.

'The stupendous size of the shafts of these columns (for they are six feet in diameter, and sixty feet in height) does not more arrest the attention of the spectator than the circumstance of there being no fallen ruins on or near the spot, which was covered with one hundred and twenty columns, and the marble walls of a temple abounding in statues of gods and heroes, and a thousand offerings of splendid piety.

'The solitary grandeur of these marble ruins is, perhaps, more striking than the appearance presented by any other object at Athens; and the Turks themselves seem to regard them with an eye of respect and veneration.'

John Cam Hobhouse, *A Journey through Albania and Other Provinces of Turkey in Europe*, 1813

The Monument of Lysicrates, a small marble rotunda dating from the fourth century BC, *was popular with visitors not only for its graceful proportions, but also because of its Byronic associations.*

'The Choragic monument, formerly called the Lantern of Demosthenes . . . was in the garden of the Franciscan monastery, and was used by the monks as a summer-house. Lord Byron, when a resident with the fathers, made it his study. There is just room in it for a small chair and a very small table. The convent is now pulled down, the garden devastated, and this beautiful little specimen of Greek art stands in a waste place. The old marble panels have been replaced between the pillars, and on one of these is still legible the name of BYRON, – the autograph of the great poet. This was but one, though perhaps the most beautiful, of many monuments of the same kind. Two pillars stand by the outer wall of the Acropolis, which have borne tripods; and a portion of the basement is still remaining on the top of the ''Lantern'', whereupon the ancient tripod was placed.'

The Rev. Henry Christmas, *The Shores and Islands of the Mediterranean*, 1851

38 Alfred Beaumont, *The Choragic Monument of Lysicrates*, 1834

Hadrian's Gate stands on the west side of the Olympieum.

'The arch which was built in the time of Hadrian was not one of the gates of Athens, being considerably within its ancient peribolos. Little remains to be said upon a monument which has not much architectural merit, and which has been scrupulously detailed by Stuart. The inscriptions in iambic verse, which are on each side, indicate the situations of the old town, or Theseiopolis, and of new Athens, or Hadrianopolis. The former contained the space which includes the Acropolis, extending beyond the Musaeum and the Pnyx, and towards the Academy. The latter occupied a part of the plain between the Ilissos and Anchesmos.'

Edward Dodwell, *A Classical and Topographical Tour through Greece*, 1819

39 Ippoliti Caffi, *Hadrian's Gate*, 1844

The Odeum of Herodes Atticus, to the south of the Acropolis, was built in the second century AD to serve as both theatre and concert-hall.

'The theatre, or Odeion, which is at the south-west angle of the Acropolis, joins the rock into which the seats of the Κοῖλον were cut. It has only two κερκίδες, or *precinctiones*; one at the top, the other near the middle: its western side unites with the modern walls of the Acropolis. The Turks have increased its height by the addition of some modern work, – which they have perforated with loop holes, for muskets. Wheler, Spon, and Stuart, are of opinion that this is the theatre of Bacchus; but Barthelemy thinks that it is the Odeion of Herodes Atticus . . . and there can be little doubt that it is the Odeion built by Herodes Atticus, in honour of his wife Regilla.'

40 Ippolito Caffi, *The Theatre of Herodes Atticus*, 1843

Edward Dodwell, *A Classical and Topographical Tour through Greece*, 1819

The west gate of the Roman Agora, the Gate of Athena Archegetis (she who governs), was erected between 11 and 9 BC. During the Turkish period it was called 'Pazaroporta' (Bazaar Gate) because of its vicinity to the market.

'The gate of the Agora, or new market, [is] formed by four fluted Doric pillars supporting a pediment, near which stands Adrian's market tariff, as legible, and almost as perfect as the day it was placed there.'

Edward Giffard, *A Short Visit to the Ionian Islands, Athens, and the Morea*, 1838

42 Ippolito Caffi, *The Agora Gate*, 1843

144

41 Thomas Hartley Cromek, *The Hill of the Areopagus*, 1846

After a tour of the Acropolis, the visitor could climb the hill of Mars, or the Areopagus, the most ancient tribunal of Greece, where Orestes was tried for matricide, and Socrates for atheism, and where St Paul preached the new religion of Christianity to the pagan Greeks.

'The Areopagus is situated a few hundred feet west of the Acropolis. It consists in an insulated rock, precipitous, and broken towards the south; on the north side it slopes gently down towards the temple of Theseus, and is rather lower than the Acropolis. Its even summit in several places is flattened and cut into steps, but not a fragment of any ancient building remains. Some steps are also cut in the rock on the southern side.'

Edward Dodwell, *A Classical and Topographical Tour through Greece*, 1819

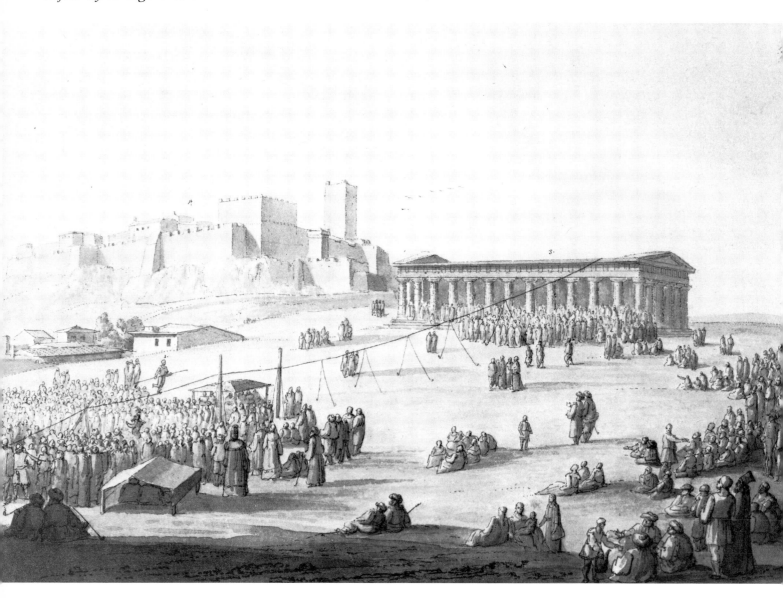

43 Sebastiano Ittar, *Fête with a Tightrope Walker by the Theseum*, 1800

In the nineteenth century the area around the Theseum was used for festivals.

'This morning I strolled to the temple of Theseus . . . Nothing can be more orderly than a Greek mob. There were about two thousand persons here; and although they were boisterous in their mirth, there was nothing mischievous in it. They were like a parcel of children, dancing with all the animation imaginable, to the sound of the drum and the pipe.'

George Cochrane, *Wanderings in Greece*, 1837

'The national dance of the Romaika is an amusement to which the Greeks appear to be devoted. In every part of the country . . . I have seen circles of white-kilted men, and occasionally women, joining in the popular dance to the music of drum and fife, or an instrument like the German zither. The dancers who form the ring are generally linked together by holding on to bright-coloured handkerchiefs . . . In the middle of the ring, sometimes a man alone, sometimes a man and a woman, execute the most marvellous steps until exhausted, when their place is taken by fresh dancers.'

Frederick Trench Townshend, *A Cruise in Greek Waters*, 1870

'A ramble through the city of Athens in any direction, must be pursued, through a confused assemblage of well-built houses of recent construction, of miserable houses raised among the ruins of former habitations, and of ruined churches and houses . . . In the midst of the latter you may frequently observe some half-buried column or massive fragment of an antique wall or foundation thrown into bolder relief by the mean and insignificant proportions of the remains. This anomalous [combination] of two epochs, of the past with the present, so widely different from both, is a peculiarity which will awake the imagination of the least speculative.'

William Page, inscription on verso of pl. 27 (see p. 121)

44 Joseph Scherer, *Greek Dance in Athens*, 1849

45 J. P. E. F. Peytier, *An Athenian Quarter*, 1833

In 1833 the Bavarian Prince Otho was appointed King of Greece by the Great Powers. Soon after his arrival in Athens, great attempts were made in order to give a European aspect to the new Hellenic capital. The picturesque combination of new Neoclassical buildings, ruined Turkish houses and classical edifices surprised the European visitors of the late 1850s who found in Athens modern buildings, 'rather German in appearance', springing up on every side.

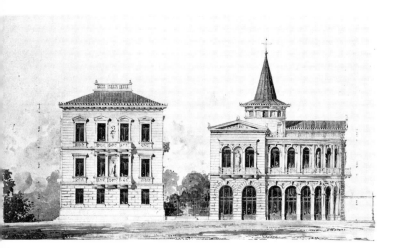

46 Ernst Ziller, *Designs for Two Athenian Villas*, 1895

47 Leo von Klenze, *Project for the Church of St Dionysius Areopagites*, 1844

The church of St Dionysius Areopagites, the Roman Catholic Cathedral, is considered among the finest examples of Neoclassical religious architecture in Greece. Designed by Leo von Klenze in 1844, it was built with slight alterations between 1858 and 1888 by the Greek architect Lyssandros Kaftantzoglou.

'The buildings dating from this period, whether with plain or richly decorated façades, retain nonetheless their essential constructional character. The stone or marble base of the building, the marble staircase and the portal of the entrance constitute the basic elements, together with the balconies with their highly decorative balustrades and buttresses. Additionally, a typical element of Athenian buildings, even the humbler ones, is the highly-ornate anthemion-shaped clay roof tiles which crown the top of the façade like a garland.'

John Travlos, *Neoclassical Architecture in Greece*, 1967

48 Wilhelm von Weiler, *The Central Hospital, Athens*, 1836

'The great square before the Palace is called of the Syntagma, or Constitution, for the convenience of the King. The Greeks take a Constitution seriously – almost as seriously as our House of Lords . . . Democracy makes the charm of the square. On a spring evening, ere the sea side has come into vogue, you may see any and every Athenian type sitting cheek by jowl with any other, or strolling up and down among a motley gathering of diplomatists, tourists, and figures from the Levant lands. Family parties or groups of friends sit happily round little tables, justifying their occupation with perhaps only one *consommation* among the lot, perhaps with none at all. But no-one cares . . . Outwardly, it is a sombre crowd, for aspiring Greece wears black coat and black hat, and only rarely may you see the starched *fustanella* kilt, blue gaiters, broidered zouave and vest, and soft red-tasselled cap, which the exploits of the Suliotes and the vanity of King Otho imposed as a national dress.'

Scenes in Athens . . . Described by David Hogarth, c. 1900

'We then continued our walk to the military hospital, on the eastern side of the acropolis. This is a building worthy of any capital in the world. It is constructed with great taste, and has a striking effect as viewed from the sea; for immediately on observing the columns of the temple of Jupiter, you cannot avoid being attracted by this building. It will contain two hundred beds.'

George Cochrane, *Wanderings in Greece,* 1837

49 Giorgio Peritelli, *Syntagma (Constitution) Square,* 1863

'The main street, which runs northward from the Acropolis through the heart of the medieval and modern town, is named after the God of the Winds . . . It is the most attractive of all athenian streets . . . The shops in it are mean enough for the most part, as shops in a city without commerce are apt to be; but, at the southern end especially, they retain some semblance of that earlier *bazaar* form which is proper to the place. Here, where little wheeled traffic attempts to pass, because the rock-wall of the Acropolis makes the streets something of a blind alley, men and children lead their lives mainly without the houses, and the women hang, as is their custom in Greek lands, out of the upper windows, shrilly passing the time of day. Merchandise overflows the pavement and fills the gutter, and the most intimate attentions of mother to child, or man to man, go on in the view of the sun and the public . . . But the matchless feature of the street, seen from end to end of it, is that tremendous battlemented steep of the Acropolis, a frowning rampart of dark rock, heightened above by the orange tint of the wall and glimpses of marbles on the summit. Aeolus Street is not the finest street even in Athens, but it leads you straight up to the finest site in the world.'

Scenes in Athens . . . Described by David Hogarth, c. 1900

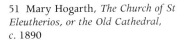

50 Mary Hogarth, *The Athenian Market in Aeolus Street, c. 1890*

The church of St Eleutherios, or Panaghia Gorgoepikoos, dates from the twelfth century. Its richly decorated fresco interior was destroyed in 1862. During the Othonian period it was used as a temporary museum of antique inscriptions.

'The smallest of Athenian churches is, curiously enough, the old Cathedral, seat of the Metropolitan until some years later than the liberation, but now superseded by the new basilica on its northern flank. Once closely beset by the *bazaar*, this gem of byzantine architecture now stands free to the admiration of all who pass directly between the great square and the western end of the Acropolis. The walls are composed of antique blocks, many of them inscribed and some bearing reliefs . . . the whole structure is a marvel of miniature proportions and mellow tones.'

Scenes in Athens . . . Described by David Hogarth, c. 1900

51 Mary Hogarth, *The Church of St Eleutherios, or the Old Cathedral, c. 1890*

During the years of the Turkish occupation the port of Piraeus was almost deserted. It was then known as Porto Draco or Porto Leone, after the colossal marble statue of a lion that stood at the entrance to the port (the statue was transported to Venice in 1687 by the Venetian General Morosini). After the War of Revolution the modern town of Piraeus was founded in 1834 by settlers from Hydra, Syros and Scio.

52 Ludwig Köllnberger, *The Custom House in Piraeus*, 1837

'The Piraeus . . . contains a great number of houses; its streets are properly laid out; its municipality is organized; and there is every hope of its being a place of great commercial importance. . . . Most of the houses at the Piraeus belong to Hydriotes, and they are consequently well built and well painted . . . the custom-house, a very fine large building . . . is intended, not merely for the transit, but the deposit of goods, until means are found of sending them to other markets.'

George Cochrane, *Wanderings in Greece*, 1837

One of the most popular sites with nineteenth-century visitors was the Temple of Poseidon at Sunium, then known as the Temple of Minerva Sunias. Superbly located on the southernmost tip of Attica, the temple possessed the added attraction of Byron's signature on one of its columns.

53 Joseph Mallord William Turner,
The Temple of Minerva at Sunium,
1832

'This temple, elevated on high above the Aegaean Sea, at the extremity of this promontory, stood like the Portico or Vestibule of Attica. Constructed of white marble, placed on this noble site, and visible at a great distance from the sea, it reminded the stranger who approached it in his vessel from the south, by the fair proportions of its architecture, and by the decorations of sculpture and of painting with which it was adorned, that he was coming to a land illustrious for its skill in the most graceful Arts; a land set apart, as it were, from all others for their cultivation, and appropriated to their use; and that as this fabric, dedicated to Minerva, was approached by a portico, and surrounded by a consecrated enclosure, so the whole land of ATTICA itself was a sacred TEMENOS, whose boundaries were Seas and Moutains, and whose PROPYLAEA was the Temple of Minerva on the promontory of Sunium.'

Christopher Wordsworth, *Greece: Pictorial, Descriptive and Historical,* 1839

'Ask the traveller what strikes him as most poetical, – the Parthenon, or the rock on which it stands? The COLUMNS of Cape Colonna or the Cape itself? . . . There are a thousand rocks and capes far more picturesque than those of the Acropolis and Cape Sunium in themselves; what are they to a thousand scenes in the wilder parts of Greece, of Asia Minor, Switzerland, or even of Cintra in Portugal, or to many scenes of Italy, and the Sierras of Spain? But it is the *"art"*, the columns, the temples, the wrecked vessel, which give them their antique and their modern poetry, and not the spots themselves. Without them, the *spots* of the earth would be unnoticed and unknown.'

Byron, *Letter . . . on the Rev. W. L. Bowles's Strictures on the Life and Writings of Pope*, 1821

54 William Henry Bartlett, *The Temple of Minerva at Cape Colonna*, late 1830s

The Peloponnesus

'Though the surface of the Peninsula is only about one-third more extensive than that of Yorkshire, there is probably no part of the world which will more fully repay a tour of a month or six weeks. The scenery, both of the great historic sites and of the more obscure retreats of the Peloponnese, is of the rarest grandeur and beauty, and stamps itself on the memory with distinctness. Other sights and length of time do not confuse or alter its impressions. The cloud-capped Acropolis of Corinth, the primaeval remains of Tiryns and Mykenae, the hollow stadium-like valley of Sparta, . . . the mountain-shrine of Bassae, the beautiful vale of Olympia, . . . all these are among the choice places of the earth which, once seen, live in perpetual freshness in the imagination.'

John Murray, *A Handbook for Travellers in Greece*, 1872

55 Karl Wilhelm von Heydeck, *View of Nafplion*, 1834

Nafplion, with its excellent harbour and naturally fortified acropolis, is situated on the shore of the Gulf of Argolis. The city was named Nauplia in antiquity, Nauplion in the Byzantine period, then Anapli and Napoli di Romania by the Venetians.

'Nauplia became the seat of Government soon after it fell into the hands of the Greeks, and continued such, until his Hellenic Majesty removed his royal residence to Athens, in December, 1834. The excellence of its port and the strength of its fortress were the causes that made Nauplia so long the capital of Greece; but since the removal of the government, it has greatly fallen off in prosperity and has not now much trade. . . . Several interesting excursions may be made from Nauplia and a traveller may spend a week here agreeably, previous to commencing his tour in the Peloponnesus.'

John Murray, *A Handbook for Travellers in Greece*, 1854

'The *Fortress of the Palamede* stands on the summit of a lofty and precipitous rock, 720 feet above the level of the sea. It is inaccessible on all sides except at one point to the E., where it is connected with a range of barren, rocky hills, and was surnamed the Gibraltar of Greece. It has been deemed impregnable, and would probably be so with any other garrison than Greeks and Turks. The former, in fact, only obtained possession of it by blockade, and when all the Turkish gunners on the hill, having been reduced by famine to 7, descended to the town by night in search of provisions, the Greeks approached and took possession of it; and the standard of the Cross floated on the summit during the remainder of the war.'

John Murray, *A Handbook for Travellers in Greece*, 1854

56 Karl Krazeisen, *View of Fort Palamede at Nafplion*, 1834

57 Théodore du Moncel, *View of Mycenae*, 1843

58 Otto Magnus von Stackelberg, *The Lion Gate at Mycenae*, 1812

Travellers to Nafplion were eager to visit the nearby site of Mycenae, which was considered one of the greatest archaeological wonders of the world. It was not until 1876 that Heinrich Schliemann's excavations brought to light the legendary treasures described by Homer, but visitors earlier in the century could trace the main outlines of the citadel and its monumental entrance, the Lion Gate, built c. 1250 BC.

'The ruins of Mycenae . . . are in some respects unequalled in interest by any object in Greece. Their position is fortunate; there is no habitation on the spot, and you rise from a vacant plain to the deserted hill upon which they stand. The citadel occupied an eminence stretching from east to west, and supplying a platform of about a thousand feet in length and half that distance in breadth. Three mountain-torrents, coming from the hills on the east, flowed in their rocky beds, one on the north, the other on the south, along the foot of the Acropolis, and thence were carried into the general receptacle of the neighbouring mountain streams, the Argolic plain. The walls of the citadel may be traced in their entire circuit, and on the western side they rise to a considerable height. The interior of their enclosure, or area of the citadel, is covered with the common turf and mountain-plants of the country. Only a few foundations of ancient buildings remain . . . Such is the present state of the Acropolis of Mycenae.'

Christopher Wordsworth, *Greece: Pictorial, Descriptive and Historical*, 1839

'Crossing a barren valley, I saw the ruins of Mycenae on the side of a facing hill. I particularly admired one of the gates of the city fashioned out of gigantic blocks of stone that are set on the rock of the mountain itself and seem to form part of it. Two colossal lions carved on each side of the gate are its only ornament; these are represented in relief and stand on their hind legs looking outwards, like the lions which support the coats of arms of our knights of old. The heads of the lions are missing. Not even in Egypt have I seen such imposing architecture, and the desert which surrounds it adds still further to its grandeur.'

François René de Chateaubriand, *Itinéraire de Paris à Jérusalem*, 1811

156

A short distance south of the citadel at Mycenae the visitor came upon the royal tomb known as the 'Treasury of Atreus' which had survived intact from the thirteenth century BC.

'The Cyclopean ruins are found frequently enough in Greece and in Italy, but the most remarkable of all are those of Mycenae and Tiryns which are even more interesting because, when wandering through them, Pausanias under arm, one finds them in more or less the same state in which that celebrated traveller of antiquity saw them seventeen centuries ago.

'Apart from the acropolis, whose outlines can be followed in their entirety, there still exists at Mycenae an astonishingly well-preserved treasury, which Pausanias mentions under the name of the Treasury of Atreus . . .'

Théodore du Moncel, *De Venise à Constantinople à travers la Grèce, c.* 1843

59 Edward Dodwell, *Interior of the Treasury of Atreus*, 1834

At Nemea, a few miles north-west of Mycenae, three solitary columns from the Temple of Jupiter were all that remained of the ancient sanctuary. It was here that the Nemean Games, one of the four great Panhellenic Festivals of ancient Greece, were held.

'It was a calm, beautiful evening . . . I seated myself on a block of marble in the centre of the most prominent heaps of rubbish, to take a general survey of this scene of desolation and to watch the last beams of expiring light gradually becoming fainter and fainter behind the surrounding hills . . . these are dark and rocky in the surface, yet less bold in their outline . . . The site was profoundly melancholy as well as from its tranquil features, as from the contrast between the present state of so celebrated a spot, and the scene it once represented . . . Not a single village, house or living creature was to be seen – not a tree or shrub . . . Never in any spot was the feeling of desolation so profoundly brought into the mind.'

William Page, inscription on verso of pl. 60

60 William Page, *The Temple of Zeus in Nemea*, 1820

61 Edward Lear, *View of Sparta from the Ancient Theatre*, 1849/80

Following the road south from Nafplion to Sparta, the traveller could enjoy splendid views of the Laconian plain, and of the mountain ranges of Parnon and Taygetus. Crossing the Eurotas, he found himself at Lacedaemon, of which almost nothing had survived. From the thirteenth century, when the town was abandoned in favour of Mistras, until the new town of Sparta was founded by King Otho in the late 1830s, the site of ancient Sparta had remained deserted.

'What a beautiful sight! But how sad it was! The solitary Eurotas flowing under the remains of the Babyx bridge, ruins everywhere, and not a soul among them. I stood motionless, in a sort of stupor, contemplating the scene. . . . A deep silence surrounded me. I wanted at least to hear an echo speak in these surroundings where there was no sound of any human voice. So I shouted with all my strength: Leonidas! None of the ruins repeated that great name. Even Sparta seemed to have forgotten it.'

François René de Chateaubriand, *Itinéraire de Paris à Jérusalem*, 1811

Five miles from Sparta, the hill of Mistras offered the most exquisite views over the Lacedaemonian plain.

'The modern town of Mistras, built by the Turks on the slopes of the mountain, is still one of the most considerable in the Peloponnesus. Above groves of olive-trees and cypresses, these last often of enormous size, rise the watchtowers intended for the defence of the town, and the minarets of the mosques. The mountain-range of Taygetus, which stretches away to the right, extends as far as the Gulf of Laconia, bordering the vast plain of the Eurotas to the west. Streams gush from the deep fissures which score the plain. Beyond the nearest of these fissures, which divides the town in two, lies the district of Perora with its houses and trees scattered in picturesque groups.'

62 Otto Magnus von Stackelberg, *View of Mistras*, 1812

Otto Magnus von Stackelberg, *La Grèce. Vues pittoresques et topographiques*, 1834

'Mistras is a modern town. Travellers used to think that it was the same as ancient Sparta, but how would it be possible to recognize the city of Lycurgus in one whose architecture presents such a confusing mélange of styles, Oriental, Gothic, Greek and Italian? It is probable that Mistras owes its origin to the French, for it was founded in 1207 by Guillaume de Ville-Hardouin . . . The lower part of the city, where one sees many church-towers, some minarets, and cypresses forming pyramids of verdure, is crowned by a castle . . . situated on the very top of a conical rock that is the last echelon of Mount Taygetus. This ensemble is of the most remarkable character. The Gothic tower is in ruins. All is abandoned. Although it is a modern city, some antiquities from the ruins of nearby Sparta can be found there, because the conquerors who built this city used the materials which they found at hand for their fortresses and principal edifices.'

Expédition scientifique de Morée, 1831–8

63 Prosper Baccuet, *View of Mistras*, 1831

64 Edward Dodwell, *The Temple of Apollo at Bassae*, 1806

The highlight of a tour of Arcadia in the central Peloponnesus was a visit to Bassae. This was the site of the celebrated Temple of Apollo Epicurius whose very existence had been forgotten until it was rediscovered by the French traveller Bocher in 1765. From the summit of the temple the traveller could enjoy unrivalled views over the Messenian Gulf.

'''Phigalia is encompassed with mountains. Kotylion is on the left, and Elaïon advances on its right. Kotylion is forty stadia from the city. Upon this mountain there is a place called Bassai, with the Temple of Apollo Epicurius, the roof of which is of marble. This temple is more admired than any in the Peloponnesos, after that at Tegea, both on account of the beauty of its stone and the harmony of its structure. The name of Ἐπικούριος, or the Helper, was given to Apollo, from the aid which he afforded to the inhabitants in a pestilential malady. Iktinos, who built the Parthenon, was also the architect of this temple.'' [Pausanias] . . .

'The view from the temple is particularly attractive, from the beauty of the lines and the interest of the objects. The distant mountain on the left of the view is Taygeton. The nearer range is Lycaeon and Karausios, above the lower part of which the eye glances upon the Messenian Gulf, the memorable plain of Stenyklaros, and the flat-topped Ithome. On the right-hand side of the view the plain of Cyparissiai is seen between the columns, and the horizon is bounded by the gulf of Cyparissiai and the Sicilian sea.'

65 Edward Lear, *The Temple of Apollo at Bassae*, 1854/55

Edward Dodwell, *Views in Greece*, 1821

66 Otto Magnus von Stackelberg,
View of Andritsaina, 1812

*Descending from Bassae, the traveller would stop at the picturesque town of
Andritsaina.*

'This charming little town of Arcadia is situated upon two hills in front of
Mount Cotylion . . . Pretty houses, and springs running under the shady and
beautiful trees which decorate the roads and paths, make it very attractive. It is
surrounded by numerous orchards, amongst which rise cypresses; a gigantic
plane-tree decorates the public square. On a small hill a church and a convent
can be seen . . . Leaving the city, one appreciates at a glance all the sinuous
complexity of the little valleys, defiles, and chains of mountains which cross on
all sides and rise almost imperceptibly up to Mounts Pholoe, Erymanthi and
Aroania. The River Alpheus flows through the small valleys. The city is
governed by Greek Archontes, the Turks never having been established there,
which explains the happy and peaceful situation of the inhabitants.'

Otto Magnus von Stackelberg, *La Grèce. Vues pittoresques et topographiques*, 1834

Corinth was the final stage of a tour of the Peloponnesus; the traveller would cross the Isthmus and then follow the road along the Saronic Gulf to return to Athens. Despite the prosperity of Corinth in classical times, it was subsequently destroyed many times throughout its history. After the War of Independence hardly a building in the town was left standing.

'On a marvellously riven outcrop of stone, the old citadel, the Acrocorinthus, stands out against a blue sky. At its feet, along a rocky ledge, lie the houses of new Corinth.

'Once, in the legendary past, the old citadel was the centre of flourishing life and activity, and the city held incalculable treasures. Heroes, orators and poets were lauded in passionate song. Magnificent temples arose, their sanctuaries adorned with divine images of inimitable beauty.

'Now the fair countryside is impoverished, the ground is stony, the city reduced to penury, the inhabitants sorrowful and oppressed. Few ships now sail into the harbour, and the marketplace, through which the merchandise of the East once passed to the West, is half-deserted.'

Otto Magnus von Stackelberg, *Trachten und Gebräuche der Neugriechen*, 1831

67 Otto Magnus von Stackelberg,
The Bazaar of Corinth, 1812

68 William Cole, *The Temple of Apollo at Corinth*, 1833

The Temple of Apollo at Corinth, built in the sixth century BC, *is situated on a rocky terrace dominating the site of the Roman Agora.*

'These seven columns are the only existing monuments of the once celebrated and renowned city of Corinth. The materials are of rough, porous stone; the shafts of the columns are each of one block only, and the whole has been covered with stucco. . . . Byron has described these ruins, and the scenery around them, in several parts of his "Siege of Corinth" . . . The situation of the Temple commands a beautiful view, looking upon the Gulf of Lepanto; and the mountains of Parnassus, Helicon and Cithaeron, are distinctly seen.'

William Cole, *Select Views of the Remains of Ancient Monuments in Greece*, 1835

The Aegean Islands

A tour of the islands of the Aegean would be undertaken by those who possessed the time and inclination to deviate from the tourist's conventional itinerary. Most of the islands offered only limited facilities to the nineteenth-century visitor; and on those which were renowned in antiquity, such as Crete and the Cyclades, little had yet been excavated. Travellers, therefore, usually spent a few hours on each, and, while cruising among them, would enjoy the variety of their forms and the clarity of their outlines.

'The appearance of most of the Aegean Islands, on first approaching them, is exceedingly similar. Instead of the rich verdure and fragrant groves of Corfu and Zante, they generally present at a distance rude cliffs and verdureless acclivities, whose uniformity is scarcely broken by a single tree, and whose loneliness is seldom enlivened by a village or a human habitation. . . . On landing, however, every islet presents a different aspect; and every secluded hamlet a new picture of life, of manners, of costume, and sometimes of dialect.'

John Murray, *A Handbook for Travellers in Greece*, 1854

'The currents of the tideless sea glide wavelessly around their shores, and the rays of the unclouded sun beam fiercely down on their unsheltered hills . . . The soil of one is rich, and luxurious, and verdant; that of a second, only a few miles distant, is dry, scorched, and volcanic; the harbour of another is filled with the little trading craft of all the surrounding ports; its quays rife with the hum and hurry of commerce, and its coffee-houses crowded with the varied inhabitants of a hundred trading-marts; whilst a fourth . . . will be as quiet and noiseless as a city of the plague; its shores unvisited, its streets untrodden, and its fields untilled.'

James Emerson, *Letters from the Aegean*, 1829

69 Ludwig Lange, *A Dovecote in Tenos*, 1835

The Peloponnesus

XXIII William Linton, *View of the Town of Arcadia (Kyparissia)*, 1840

The town of Arcadia, on the west coast of the Peloponnesus, was built on the site of ancient Kyparissia. It was largely destroyed during the War of Independence.

'The castellated town of Arkadia rising from the olivegroves on the left, displays a Claude-like composition – the bay of Arkadia completing the picture . . . In this view the modern town lies below the spectator, the ancient acropolis (where Hellenic foundations are still to be seen, on which stands a dismantled castle of the middle ages), occupies the centre of the picture and rises to the horizontal line; the great bay of Arkadia ascending the left of the scene to the extreme distance, in which the mountains of Elis are conspicuous.'

William Linton, *The Scenery of Greece and its Islands*, 1856

XXIV Karl Rottmann, *View of the Plain of Olympia with the River Alpheus*, 1835

The first systematic excavations of ancient Olympia, site of the chief sanctuary of Zeus in Greece and of the Olympic Games held in his honour, were carried out by members of the French Scientific Expedition to the Morea in May 1829. In 1875 a treaty ratified by the Greek Parliament authorized Germany to undertake a complete excavation of the site.

'We set out at eight o'clock on a fine morning, keeping to the right bank of the Alpheus. The mountains, covered with sometimes beautiful specimens of spruce and pine, fell away and the valley broadened out.

'After an hour a hollow appeared in the side of the mountain along which we were travelling. This opened out into a large enclosed area bordered by sparse, wooded hills . . . Two trenches marked the excavations of the French expedition: traces of enormous walls, some huge upturned stones, and a fluted column base of colossal girth were all that remained of ancient Olympia.'

Gustave Flaubert, *Voyage en Orient*, 1849–51

XXV William Page, *View of Corinth with the Acrocorinthus*, 1820

Until the middle of the nineteenth century, the greater part of the town of Corinth presented a picture of desolation. The visitor was nonetheless recompensed by the majestic sight of the Acrocorinthus, girdled at the summit by the massive walls of the Venetian fortress.

'This City has been called the Gibraltar of Greece . . . On the south stands the magnificent hill, which served as the citadel of the place for 3000 years, and was called by the ancient inhabitants Acrocorinthus . . . The Acrocorinthus is by far the most striking object I have ever seen either at home or abroad . . . It stands nearly insulated, in the midst of the plain . . . a colossal mass of rugged rock that can hardly in itself be called picturesque, although from a distance it enters into fine composition with the lines of the surrounding landscape . . .'

William Page, inscription on verso of pl. XXV

XXIII

XXIV

XXV

XXVII

XXVIII

XXIX

Swansea
28 May 1864
5. 30 — 6. P.m.

176

XXX

The Aegean Islands

XXVI Hugh William Williams, *The Temple of Jupiter Panhellenius (Aphaea) in Aegina*, 1820

The Temple of Aphaea at Aegina was built towards the end of the fifth century BC. *Its famous sculptures were unearthed in 1811 by an international expedition which included the English architect Charles Robert Cockerell and the German scholar Baron Haller von Hallerstein.*

'On ascending the hill on which the temple [of Jupiter Panhellenius] stands, our way was disputed by hugh loose stones, dwarf pine and cedar trees: . . . We seated ourselves on a fallen capital, to recover a little from our fatigue, before we ventured to examine the Doric ruins, and we could not but admire the glorious scene before us; Attica, Peloponnesus, and the Gulf of Aegina, with their many points of attraction, addressing both the eye and mind! . . .'

Hugh William Williams, *Travels in Italy, Greece and the Ionian Islands*, 1820

XXVII Alexandre Gabriel Decamps, *A House in Syros, c.* 1823

The island of Syros owed its importance mainly to its port, Hermoupolis, which was founded by Greek refugees from Chios and Psara after the Revolution.

XXVIII Karl Rottmann, *View of Santorini with the Volcano*, 1835

Santorini (Thera) and the islands in the vicinity were formed by volcanic eruption.

XXIX Edward Lear, *View of Chania, Crete*, 1864

Crete was under Venetian rule for five centuries, until it was captured by the Turks in 1669. It did not subsequently gain its autonomy until 1898. Chania became the administrative capital of Crete in 1841.

'Khania, the second city of Crete at the time of the Venetians, is now its capital . . . It is an over-crowded town, as it was in the time of the Venetians, from the narrowness of the streets, the height of some of the houses and the confined limits of the original plan . . . In looking towards the south from the bay . . . the peaks of the noble mass of the Madara Vouna, the ancient Leuci or White Mountains, rise most picturesquely before one in a serrated arch, whose summits, after midsummer, appear bald and grey, but in winter and spring are covered with snow . . .'

Captain T. A. B. Spratt, *Travels and Researches in Crete*, 1865

XXX Thomas Hope, *View of Naxos with the Portico of the Temple of Bacchus, c.* 1795

Naxos, the largest of the Cyclades, was in mythology the island where Theseus deserted Ariadne. During the Middle Ages the island formed the Duchy of Naxos, an independent state under the protection of Venice.

'Being unable to undertake a journey into the interior, we next visited the ruins of a Temple of Bacchus, upon an insular rock on the north side of the port. . . . We were struck with admiration at the massive structure and the simple grandeur of that part of the temple which still remains standing: it consists of three pieces only of the *Naxian* marble, two being placed upright and one laid across. . . . The view through this portal, of the town of Naxos with its port, and part of the island, is very fine . . .'

Edward Daniel Clarke, *Travels in Various Countries of Europe, Asia and Africa*, 1810–23

The island of Salamis opposite the Piraeus was mainly of historical interest, since it was the site of the famous naval victory of the Athenians over the Persians in 480 BC.

'The greater part of Salamis is in an uncultivated state, and covered with bushes; but this is probably to be attributed to the scanty population rather than to the natural barrenness of the soil. It is inhabited only by Greeks, who enjoy a good deal of liberty . . . The capital, as well as the island itself, is at present known by the name of Koloura, from the form of its port, which resembles a round cake called by that name, and made at Athens.'

Edward Dodwell, *A Classical and Topographical Tour through Greece*, 1819

70 William James Muller, *View of the Island of Salamis*, 1838

The island of Aegina in the Saronic Gulf was of great archaeological interest, and could easily be visited from Athens in a day. A place of refuge during the Greek War of Independence, it became the seat of government of Capodistrias in 1828.

71 Karl Krazeisen, *View of Aegina*, 1826

'The island of Aegina, without being one of the most fertile of the Archipelago, is, however, because of its position, one of the most agreeable and most interesting . . . The new town of Aegina is built on the actual site of ancient Aegina, and for the most part with the same material of those old walls and tombs which abound there . . . The view . . . shows the isthmus of Corinth in the background with the mountains extending on the right towards Athens and on the left towards the Morea. The middle of the picture is occupied by the city and the port. Above the city can be seen the sole surviving column of the temple of Neptune.'

Karl Krazeisen, *Bildnisse ausgezeichneter Griechen und Philhellenen nebst einigen Ansichten und Trachten*, 1828–31

In the seventeenth century Hydra was a place of refuge for persecuted Christians from mainland Greece. From the mid-eighteenth century the island enjoyed a great prosperity based on maritime trade. During the Wars of Independence Hydra provided most of the ships for the Greek forces.

'On a rock, so utterly barren and hopeless of vegetation, that . . . I can scarcely discover, on its whole surface, one speck of verdure, rises in dazzling whiteness and beauty this singularly interesting city. . . . The harbour, from the abrupt sides and bottom of which the town starts up theatrically, is neither spacious nor secure. It is, in fact, a deep bay, situated on the western side of the island, and still open to the west, having no nearer protection from that quarter than the opposite coast of the Morea, which may be four or five miles distant. "What a place you have chosen, – (I addressed myself to Tomabazi, late Admiral of the Greek fleet,) – What a spot you have chosen for your country!" "It was Liberty that chose the spot, not we," was the patriot's instant reply; and long may Liberty preserve and protect a habitation so worthy of her.'

George Waddington, *A Visit to Greece in 1823 and 1824*, 1825

72 Thomas Hope, *View of the Town and Harbour of Hydra*, c. 1795

Poros is only divided from the mainland of the Peloponnesus by a narrow channel; with its pine-forests reaching down to the water's edge and its tiny white-washed houses, it presented a most picturesque sight to the visitor. The Monastery of the Virgin at Phaneromeni dates from the eighteenth century.

73 Wilhelm von Weiler, *View of Poros with the Monastery of Phaneromeni*, 1836

74 Thomas Hope, *View of the Island and Town of Tenos*, c. 1795

'Poros . . . the ancient *Sphaeria* . . . is remarkable for its rocks of granite. It is separated from the Peloponnesus by a very narrow channel . . . The coast of the Peloponnesus in these parts abounds in oranges and lemons; the groves of the latter on the mountain are well worth a visit. At Poros, mules may be procured, on which it is easy to pass over the sand-bank into the adjacent isle of *Calauria*, where there is a large monastery, and the substructions of the temple of Neptune, in which Demosthenes expired. . . . The little town of Poros has a singular appearance, with its houses perched like sea-gulls among its dark volcanic rocks . . .

'Poros is celebrated as having been the scene of the conferences of the English, French and Russian ambassadors in 1828; on whose joint reports, the allied governments settled the basis of the new Greek monarchy.'

John Murray, *A Handbook for Travellers in Greece*, 1854

Tenos was the most Catholic of the Cyclades, having been occupied by the Venetians from the thirteenth to the early eighteenth century. After an Icon of the Virgin had been discovered there in 1824, the island also became an important centre of pilgrimage for Orthodox Christians.

'Tino . . . is one of the best cultivated islands in the Archipelago, and there is a flourishing manufactory of coarse silk-stockings and gloves. The island contains about 66 villages, all built of white stone. The town is built of white stone, and at a distance has a showy appearance . . . The fields are divided, as at Malta, by stone: the exterior presents but a rocky aspect, but the interior is a very rich soil.'

The Rev. Samuel Sheridan Wilson, *A Narrative of the Greek Mission*, 1839

181

Melos, the most westerly of the Cyclades, is formed by a mountainous volcanic mass in the shape of an irregular ring. By the early nineteenth century, plague, Turkish exactions, and lack of water had reduced the island to a near desert.

'. . . this morning we enter the port of Milo, and anchor near the head of the bay . . . To the south-west . . . towards the hills, stands the khora, or town . . . There are 25 Greek and 2 Latin churches still remaining. The ruins and the naked valley surrounded by white rocky heights, and with scarcely any vegetation except a few meagre date-trees, give the place a most dismal appearance. . . . [To] the northern shore of the harbour are the ruins of the ancient city of Melus. . . . a little eastward of a pointed hill, near the middle of the site . . . stands a church of St. Elias, and a small monastery, with a lodging for a single monk.'

Colonel William Martin Leake, *Travels in Northern Greece*, 1835

75 James Skene, *View of Melos with the Monastery of St Marina*, 1841

The island of Chios, or Scio, had been a prosperous commercial and cultural centre since the Middle Ages. After massive destruction and the massacre of its inhabitants by the Turks in 1822, it remained deserted until the end of the War of Independence. The Monastery of Nea Moni, founded in the mid-eleventh century, is one of the most important Byzantine monuments in Greece.

76 William Gell, *View of the Monastery of Nea Moni in Chios,* 1801

'All the ideas which poetic fancy can form of an earthly paradise seem here realized . . . every where you ramble through rich vineyards intermingled with fig-trees, loaded with fruit. The valleys are intersected with paths, shaded by trees, spreading over the traveller's head branches bending under the weight of lemons, oranges, and pome-granates. The inhabitants seem willing to join their efforts to add to the charms of their island. . . . The town itself is very large and populous. . . . Literature is more cultivated in Scio than perhaps in any other part of Greece; we saw here a large school, containing nearly two hundred boys – a library of about two thousand volumes attached to it. During our stay here we paid a visit to a monastery situated on the top of a hill, commanding the port where we lay, and whence the spectator has a most delightful view of the fruitful valleys of Chios, the Asiatic coast, and the curiously-formed island of Samos.'

Peter Edmund Laurent, *Recollections of a Classical Tour through Various Parts of Greece, Turkey and Italy*, 1821

77 William James Muller, *View of the Port of Rhodes*, 1838

One of the principal ports of the Eastern Aegean, Rhodes was captured from the Knights of St John of Jerusalem by Sulaiman II in 1523 and remained in Turkish hands until 1912. Because much of its architecture of the Frankish period has survived intact, it is the least Greek in appearance of the Aegean Islands.

'When landing at Rhodes, we behold for the first time the fortress which so long formed the impregnable outwork of Latin Christianity in the East, and which, though shattered by cannon and earthquakes, still presents to us one of the noblest and most instructive specimens of military architecture in the fifteenth century . . . So absorbing indeed is the charm of this first impression, so completely does it fill our imagination, that we forget for awhile the interest which belongs to Rhodes as the site of one of the great maritime republics of the ancient world, a city celebrated not less for the wisdom of its institutions than for the beauty of its architecture, the perfection of its ports and arsenals, and the strength of its defences by sea and land.'

Charles Thomas Newton, *Travels and Discoveries in the Levant*, 1865

78 P. J. Witdoeck, *View of the Street of the Knights, Rhodes*, 1825

'The street is embellished in places with coats of arms and inscriptions which are worth a close inspection. The balconies, their gratings designed to satisfy the curiosity of the Turkish women, obstruct a complete view of the street, but at the far end can be made out the Lodge where the Knights of St John used to meet to receive the orders of the Grand Master; on the left is the Church of St John, now the principal mosque of the Turks, and on the right, a little further down, is the former palace.'

Colonel Bernard Rottiers, *Description des monumens de Rhodes*, 1830

Notes to the text

The classical prelude (pp. 11–20)

1 *Acts of the Athens Archaeological Society*, 1838, p. 26. Iakovos Rizos-Neroulos (1778–1850), a Greek writer and politician, was one of the founding members of the Greek Archaeological Society.

2 See Steven Runciman, *The Last Byzantine Renaissance*, Cambridge, 1970.

3 John Mandeville, *The Voiage and Travaile . . . which Treateth of the Way to Hierusalem and of Marvayles of Inde, with Other Ilands and Countryes*, London, 1727, pp. 19–20.

4 The Florentine monk Cristoforo Buondelmonti (1380–1430), the first European to make a thorough survey of the Greek islands, settled in Rhodes in 1406. The first manuscript edition of his *Liber Insularum Archipelagi* appeared in 1420. The original manuscript was never printed, but the work survived in various manuscript copies of the fifteenth and sixteenth centuries: see E. Legrand, *C. Buondelmonti. Description des îles de l'Archipel, version grecque par un anonyme*, Paris, 1897.

5 Nicolas de Nicolay, *Les quatre premiers livres des navigations et pérégrinations orientales*, Lyon, 1567. Nicolay made a tour of the Aegean Islands in 1551.

6 See R. R. Bolgar, *The Classical Heritage*, Cambridge, 1977, ch. VII; Steven Runciman, *Mistra*, London and New York, 1980, ch. X.

7 See D. J. Geneakoplos, 'The Diaspora Greeks: the Genesis of Modern Greek National Consciousness', in Diamantouros *et al*, *Hellenism and the First Greek War of Liberation*, Institute for Balkan Studies, Thessaloniki, 1976, pp. 59–77.

8 Martinus Crusius, *Turcogrecia*, Basle, 1584.

9 Copies of the manuscript notes by Ciriaco d'Ancona (1391–1452) were published in Florence as *Kyriaci Anconitani itinerarium nunc primum ex Ms Cod. in lucem erutum*, 1742.

10 *Etat présent des nations et églises grecque, arménienne et maronite en Turquie par Sieur de la Croix*, Paris, 1684.

11 François Olivier, Marquis de Nointel, was appointed as ambassador to the Sublime Porte in 1670. His greatest diplomatic achievement was to renew the capitulations granted to France.

12 See the Comte de la Borde, *Athènes aux XVe, XVIe et XVIIe siècles*, Paris, 1854, vol. I, pp. 74–81.

13 The Russian brothers Gregory and Alexei Orloff were sent in 1770 as emissaries of Catherine the Great to incite a rising in the Peloponnesus. The insurrection ended in total disaster and the Greeks were subjected to devastating reprisals at the hands of the Albanian irregulars called in by the Turkish authorities.

14 R. Halsband (ed.), *The Complete Letters of Lady Mary Wortley Montagu*, 3 vols, Oxford, 1965–7.

The emergence of modern Greece (pp. 21–62)

1 René Canat, *La Renaissance de la Grèce antique (1820–50)*, Paris, 1911, p. 95.

2 See David Watkin, *Thomas Hope and the Neoclassical Idea*, London, 1968, ch. III.

3 The Rev. R. Tweddell, *Remains of the Late John Tweddell, Fellow of Trinity College, Cambridge*, London, 1815.

4 Robert Smirke's diary. Royal Institute of British Architects, London (CC12).

5 G. L. Taylor, *The Autobiography of an Octogenarian Architect*, London, 1870–2, vol. I, pp. 109–10.

6 See Georges Roux, *Karl Haller von Hallerstein. Le Temple de Bassae*, Strasbourg, 1976, pp. 21–2; also Emm. Protopsaltes, *Georg Christian Gropius* (in Greek), Athens, 1947.

7 On the sculptures of Aphaea (Aegina) and Phigaleia (Bassae), see J. L. C. Garnier, *L'Ile d'Egine*, Paris, 1857; A. Furtwängler, *Aegina, Das Heiligtum der Aphaia*, Munich, 1906, pp. 10–21, 176–88; E. Michon, in *Revue des études grecques*, XXV (1912), pp. 158–208, 401–26; P. Goessler, in *Archaeologiki Ephimeris*, 1937, A', pp. 69–82.

8 H. W. Williams, *Travels in Italy, Greece and the Ionian Islands*, Edinburgh, 1820, vol. II, p. 212.

9 For Elgin's artists, see A. H. Smith, 'Lord Elgin and his Collection', in *Journal of Hellenic Studies*, XXXVI (1916), pp. 173–5; W. St Clair, *Lord Elgin and the Marbles*, London, 1967, pp. 30–1 and *passim*.

10 St Clair, *Lord Elgin*, p. 89.

11 E. D. Clarke, *Travels in Various Countries of Europe, Asia and Africa*, 1810–23, vol. II, p. 483.

12 The Rev. T. S. Hughes, *Travels in Sicily, Greece and Albania*, London, 1820, vol. I, p. 270.

13 While the Anglo-Turkish alliance created special facilities for English travellers to Greece, the blockade of the Continent during the Napoleonic Wars made Greece the most popular choice for the successors of the Grand Tourists. See *The Rediscovery of Greece*, exhibition catalogue, Fine Art Society, London, 4–29 June, 1979.

14 See P. E. Legrand, 'Biographie de L. F. S. Fauvel', in *Revue archéologique*, XXX (1897), pp. 41–66, XXXI (1897), pp. 185–223; M. Raybaud, *Mémoires sur la Grèce*, Paris, 1825, vol. I, p. 242, vol. II, p. 86; H. Tregaskis, *Beyond the Grand Tour*, London, 1979, pp. 12–20.

15 See J. P. Alaux, *La Vénus de Milo et Olivier Voutier*, Paris, 1939. A great part of the antiquities in Melos were excavated and removed in 1825 by the Dutch Colonel Bernard Rottiers: see B. Rottiers, *Description des monumens de Rhodes*, Brussels, 1830.

16 For the so-called 'Homeric' problem, i.e. whether Homer ever existed or if the Homeric setting could be identified by reference to actual topography, see Albin Lesky, *Geschichte der griechischen Literatur*, Bern/Munich, 1963.

17 J. C. Hobhouse, *Journey through Albania*, London, 1813, vol. I, pp. 301–2.

18 The Comte de Forbin, *Voyage dans le Levant*, Paris, 1819, pp. 35–6.

19 A. L. Castellan, *Lettres sur la Morée*, Paris, 1808.

20 See M. P. Nilsson, *A History of Greek Religion* (trans. from the Swedish by F. J. Fielden), London, 1925; V. Scully, *The Earth, the Temple and the Gods*, Yale University Press, 1962; Ch. Karouzos, *Ancient Greek Art* (in Greek), Athens, 1972, pp. 3–30.

21 W. Haygarth, *Greece, a Poem*, London, 1814, p. 170.

22 H. W. Williams, *Travels in Italy, Greece and the Ionian Islands*, vol. II, pp. 338–9.

23 W. C. Hazlitt (ed.), *W. Hazlitt: Essays on the Fine Arts*, London, 1873, pp. 141–4.

24 W. Linton, *The Scenery of Greece and its Islands*, London, 1856, p. 68.

25 The Queen's physician Dr Henry Holland, who visited Greece in 1812–13, remarked: 'The active spirit of the Greeks, deprived in great measure of political or national objects, has taken a general direction towards commerce . . . they emigrate in considerable numbers to adjacent countries, where their activity can have more scope in the nature of the government. . . . by far the greater part of the exterior trade of Turkey, in the exchange of commodities, is carried on by Greek houses, which have residents at home, and branches in various cities of Europe, mutually aiding each other . . . Many of the merchants here [Ioannina] have extensive continental connections, which are often family ones likewise. An instance at this time occurs to me of a Greek family, with which I was intimate, where, of four brothers, one was settled at Ioannina, another at Moscow, a third at Constantinople, and the fourth in some part of Germany; all connected together in their concerns' (*Travels in the Ionian Isles, Albania, Thessaly, Macedonia, &c.*, London, 1815, pp. 148–9).

26 The French merchant and scholar Pierre Augustin Guys (1720–99) first visited Greece in 1748 and spent the last years of his life in Zante. Guys's book is the first serious survey of the customs of modern Greeks.

27 'Exoriare aliquis nostris ex ossibus ultor', Virgil, *Aeneid*, Book IV, l. 625: Dido's curse on Aeneas when abandoned by him.

28 Michaelis calls him 'the founder of scientific geography in Greece'. Leake went to Greece in 1802. In September the same year he was on board Elgin's ship, the *Mentor*, which sank off the shores of Cythera laden with marbles. In 1804 he was sent by the British government on a diplomatic and military mission to explore the west coast of Greece, to instruct the Turkish troops in the use of modern artillery and to establish friendly relations with Ali Pasha. He returned to England in 1815. He wrote the following works on Greece: *Researches in Greece*, London, 1814; *Remarks on the Language Spoken in Greece at the Present Day*, London, 1814; *Journey through Some Provinces of Asia Minor in the Year 1800*, London, 1820; *The Topography of Athens, with Some Remarks on its Antiquities*, London, 1821; *Journal of a Tour in Asia Minor, with Comparative Remarks on the Ancient and Modern Geography of That Country*, London, 1824; *Travels in Northern Greece*, 4 vols., London, 1835; *Travels in the Morea*, 3 vols, London, 1830; *Peloponnesiaca: A Supplement to Travels in the Morea*, London, 1846.

29 F. R. de Chateaubriand, *Travels in Greece, Palestine, Egypt and Barbary . . .* (trans. by F. Shoberl), London, 1811, p. 103.

30 Lord Byron, *Childe Harold's Pilgrimage. A Romaunt*, London, 1812.

31 The Islands passed from Venetian to French rule in 1797, then were successively seized by the Russo-Turkish fleet, by the French, and finally by the British in 1814. The following year, the United States of the Ionian Islands came into being, under British protection.

32 On the subject of Philhellenism, see W. St Clair, *That Greece Might Still Be Free: The Philhellenes in the War of Independence*, London, 1972 (a very extensive bibliography); S. Laskaris, 'Le Philhellénisme allemand', in *Acropole, Revue du monde hellénique*, 1935, pp. 363–71; I. K. Chassiotes, 'Spanish Philhellenism' (in Greek), in *Makedoniki Zoi*, 70 (March 1972); A. Dimaras, 'The Other British Philhellenes', in R. Clogg (ed.), *The Struggle for Greek Independence*, London, 1973.

33 *Nobles hijos de Esparta y Atenas*

De la patria la voz escuchad
Y compiendo las viles cadenas
Del combate las armas forjad.
(Quoted in I. K. Chassiotes, op. cit.)

34 Quoted in W. St Clair, *That Greece Might Still Be Free*, p. 23.

35 *Revue encyclopédique*, XXXV (1827), p. 129. For a brief account of Philhellenic pictures, see H. Honour, *Romanticism*, London, 1979, pp. 229–31.

36 For a critical account of the works exhibited at the Galerie Lebrun, see *Revue encyclopédique*, XXX (1826), pp. 578–80; also *Images du philhellénisme français (1820–40)*, exhibition catalogue, Institut français d'Athènes, 21 May–15 June, 1971, pp. 22–3.

37 Louis Dupré exhibited the following Greek works: 'Vue d'Athènes, d'après nature', 'Divers costumes faits en Grèce, d'après nature'.

38 L. Dupré, *Voyage de Venise à Constantinople*, Paris, 1825.

39 This subject was popular in France in the 1820s and 1830s. It was first treated by Delacroix in 1827.

40 A complete set of the wallpaper series is at the Benaki Museum, Athens.

41 See C. M. Woodhouse, *The Battle of Navarino*, London, 1965.

42 E. Delacroix, 'Scène de la guerre actuelle des Turcs et des Grecs' (298) – Victor Lassus, 'Les assiégés de Missolonghi' (305) – E. Devéria, 'Marc Botsaris rentre à Missolonghi' (338) – L. Dupré, 'Un Grec arborant son étendard sur les murs de Salona' (367), and various Vues, painted in Athens (336) – Meister de Goblentz, 'Officier grec enlevant un drapeau aux Turcs' (715) – J. Odevaere, 'Les derniers défenseurs de Missolonghi' (770) – M. Phalipon, 'Deux jeunes filles grecques' (813) – M. Vinchon, 'Sujet grec moderne' (1042) – M. Moreau, 'Un Grec gardant l'entrée d'un défilé' (1288) and 'Une femme grecque attendant l'issue d'un combat' (1289) – M. Prevost, 'Corinne d'après Gérard' (1303) – F. de Lansac, 'Épisode du siège de Missolonghi' (1496).

43 See S. Papadopoulos and A. Karakatsani, *Liberated Greece and the Scientific Expedition of the Morea: The Peytier Folio* (in Greek), published by The National Bank of Greece, Athens, 1971.

44 He was also accompanied by his tutor, the eminent humanist Friedrich Thiersch, an ardent Philhellene. For Thiersch's life and activities, see H. W. J. Thiersch, *Friedrich Thiersch's Leben*, 2 vols, Leipzig/Heidelberg, 1866.

The picturesque compromise (pp. 63–78)

1 For the Bavarians in Greece, see Wolf Seidl, *Bayern in Griechenland*, Munich, 1965.

2 Georg L. von Maurer, *Das griechische Volk in öffentlicher kirchlicher und privatrechtlicher Beziehung vor und nach dem Freiheitskampfe bis zum 31. Juli 1834*, Heidelberg, 1835, vol. II, pp. 39–40.

3 G. Cochrane, *Wanderings in Greece*, London, 1837, vol. I, pp. 149–51.

4 A. Miliarakis, 'A Ceremony on the Acropolis of Athens' (in Greek), in *Estia*, 447 (22 July 1884), pp. 461–7.

5 Ross wrote the following works on Greece: *Reisen auf den griechischen Inseln des Agäischen Meeres*, 2 vols, Stuttgart, 1840–3; *Reisen und Reiserouten durch Griechenland*, Berlin, 1841; *Wanderungen in Griechenland im Gefolge des Königs Otto und der Königin Amalia*, 2 vols, Halle, 1851; *Reisen nach Kos, Halikarnassos, Rhodos und der Insel Cypern*, Halle, 1852; *Erinnerungen und Mitteilungen aus Griechenland*, Berlin, 1863.

6 I. Travlos, *Neoclassical Architecture in Greece* (in Greek), Athens, 1967.

7 B. Taylor, *Travels in Greece and Russia*, New York, 1859, p. 48.

8 J. von Nordenflycht, *Briefe einer Hofdame in Athen*, Leipzig, 1845, p. 153.

9 W. H. Bartlett, *Footsteps of Our Lord and His Apostles in Syria, Greece and Italy*, London, 1850, p. 100.

10 *Art Journal*, 1851, p. 131.

11 Muller's letter from Xanthus, dated 1843 (quoted by A. Wilton in the introduction to *Classical Sites and Monuments*, exhibition catalogue, British Museum, London, 1971).

12 Alphonse de Lamartine, *Voyage en Orient*, Paris, 1835, p. 100.

13 Quoted in Canat, *La Renaissance de la Grèce antique*, p. 139.

14 See *Scenes in Athens; Drawn and Tinted by Mary Hogarth, Described by David Hogarth*, London and New York, 190[?], pl. 17, 'The Old Cathedral'.

15 The Rev. S. S. Wilson, *A Narrative of the Greek Mission; or Sixteen Years in Malta and Greece*, London, 1839, p. 250.

16 Soon after the Revolution the Greeks grouped themselves around the representatives of the Protecting Powers to form the British, French and Russian parties, the leaders of which were respectively A. Mavrokordatos, I. Kolettis and T. Kolokotronis.

17 E. About, *Greece and the Greeks of the Present Day*, London, 1855, pp. 54–5.

18 Quoted in R. Clogg, *A Short History of Modern Greece*, Cambridge, 1979.

19 In 1830 Crete was ceded to the Egyptians by the Turks, but after the defeat of Mehemet Ali in 1840 it once again passed under Turkish rule.

20 Edward Lear, letter to his sister Ann, dated Corfu, 14 May 1848 (quoted in F. M. Tsigakou, 'Edward Lear in Greece', unpublished M. Phil. thesis, University College, London, 1977, p. 33).

21 Mark Twain, *The Innocents Abroad* (1869), ch. 31.

22 See Romilly Jenkins, *The Dilessi Murders*, London, 1961.

23 See Richard Jenkyns, *The Victorians and Ancient Greece*, Oxford, 1980, p. 180.

24 John Ruskin, *Modern Painters*, 1843–60, vol. III, ch. 13, para. 4.

Bibliographical note

There is as yet no publication that provides a comprehensive account of the activities of European artists in Greece, either in the nineteenth century or previously. Moreover, many of the artists included here are not at all well-known, and in some instances it has not been possible to discover anything else about them except that which is provided by their surviving works. Full bibliographical references, where available, about the artists, their writings or works on Greece are given in the annotated catalogue of illustrations (pp. 191–204). Other references may be found in the notes to the text (pp. 187–9).

For general studies of travel literature on Greece, see:

S. H. Weber, *Voyages and Travels in the Near East during the Nineteenth Century*, Princeton, N.J., 1952
Topography and Travel in Greece, the Near East and Adjacent Regions, Previous to the Year 1801, Princeton, N.J., 1953
K. Simopoulos, *Foreign Travellers to Greece, AD 333–1821* (in Greek), 5 vols, Athens, 1970–9

Other more general historical sources are:
John Campbell and Philip Sherrard, *Modern Greece*, London, 1968
Douglas Dakin, *The Unification of Greece 1770–1923*, London, 1972
Nikos P. Mouzelis, *Modern Greece: Facets of Underdevelopment*, London, 1978
R. Clogg, *A Short History of Modern Greece*, Cambridge, 1979
A. Kokkou, *The Conservation of Antiquities in Greece and the First Museums* (in Greek), Athens, 1977

Sources of quotations

Byron, Lord, *Childe Harold's Pilgrimage. A Romaunt*, London, 1812
The Giaour, London, 1813
The Dream, 1816
Letter to ********** [John Murray], on the Rev. W. L. Bowles's Strictures on the Life and Writings of Pope, London 1821
Cartwright, Joseph, *Views in the Ionian Islands*, London, 1821
Chateaubriand, François René de, *Itinéraire de Paris à Jérusalem, et de Jérusalem à Paris*, 3 vols, Paris, 1811
Christmas, The Rev. Henry, *The Shores and Islands of the Mediterranean*, 3 vols, London, 1851
Clarke, Edward Daniel, *Travels in Various Countries of Europe, Asia and Africa*, 6 vols, London, 1810–23
Cochrane, George, *Wanderings in Greece*, 2 vols, London, 1837
Cole, William, *Select Views of the Remains of Ancient Monuments in Greece*, London, 1835
Cook, Henry, 'The Present State of the Monuments of Greece', in *The Art Journal*, London, 1851
Recollections of a Tour in the Ionian Islands, Greece and Constantinople, London, 1835
De Vere, Aubrey, *Picturesque Sketches of Greece and Turkey*, 2 vols, London, 1850
Dodwell, Edward, *A Classical and Topographical Tour through Greece during the Years 1801, 1805 and 1806*, 2 vols,

London, 1819
Views in Greece, London, 1821
Du Moncel, Théodore, *De Venise à Constantinople à travers la Grèce*, Paris, *c.* 1843
Dupré, Louis, *Voyage à Athènes et Constantinople*, Paris, 1825
Eastlake, Charles Lock, journal. Quoted in Sir Charles Lock Eastlake, *Contributions to the Literature of the Fine Arts, Second Series*, London, 1870
Emerson, James, *Letters from the Aegean*, 2 vols, London, 1829
Expédition scientifique de Morée, ordonnée par le gouvernement français, A. Blouet *et al.*, 3 vols, Paris, 1831–8
Flaubert, Gustave, *Voyage en Orient*, 1849–51
Fulleylove, John, *Greece*, London, 1906
Garston, Edgar, *Greece Revisited*, London, 1842
Giffard, Edward, *A Short Visit to the Ionian Islands, Athens, and the Morea*, London, 1838
Haygarth, William, *Greece, a Poem*, London, 1814
Hobhouse, John Cam, *A Journey through Albania and Other Provinces of Turkey in Europe*, 2 vols, London, 1813
Holland, Henry, *Travels in the Ionian Isles, Albania, Thessaly, Macedonia, &c. during the Years 1812 and 1813*, London, 1815
Hughes, The Rev. Thomas Smart, *Travels in Sicily, Greece and Albania*, 2 vols, London, 1820
Klenze, Leo von, *Aphoristische Bemerkungen gesammelt auf seiner Reise nach Griechenland*, Berlin, 1838
Krazeisen, Karl, *Bildnisse ausgezeichneter Griechen und Philhellenen nebst einigen Ansichten und Trachten*, Munich, 1828–31
Latour, Antoine de, *Voyage de S.A.R. Monseigneur le duc de Montpensier à Tunis, en Egypte, en Turquie et en Grèce*, Paris, 1847

Laurent, Peter Edmund, *Recollections of a Classical Tour through Various Parts of Greece, Turkey, and Italy, Made in the Years 1818 & 1819*, London, 1821
Leake, Colonel William Martin, *Travels in Northern Greece*, 4 vols, London, 1835
Lear, Edward, letter to his sister Ann, Athens, 3 June 1848. Quoted in F. M. Tsigakou, 'Edward Lear in Greece', unpublished M.Phil. thesis, University College, London, 1977
Journals of a Landscape Painter in Albania, &c., London, 1851
letter to his sister Ann, Corfu, 19 June 1856. From 'Edward Lear. Letters to his sister Ann, 1837–1861', typescript in the possession of Vivien Noakes
letter to Chichester Fortescue, Corfu, 9 October 1856. Quoted in Lady Strachey (ed.), *Letters of Edward Lear*, London, 1907
Views in the Seven Ionian Islands, London, 1863
Le Roy, Julien David, *Les Ruines des plus beaux monuments de la Grèce*, Paris, 1758
Linton, William, *The Scenery of Greece and its Islands*, London, 1856
Murray, John, *A Handbook for Travellers in Greece*, new edition, London, 1854
A Handbook for Travellers in Greece, 4th edition, London, 1872
Newton, Charles Thomas, *Travels and Discoveries in the Levant*, 2 vols, London, 1865
Page, William, inscription on verso of his watercolour, *View of the Acropolis, c.* 1820 (pl. 27)
inscription on verso of his watercolour, *The Temple of Zeus in Nemea*, 1820 (pl. 60)
inscription on verso of his watercolour, *View of Corinth with the Acrocorinthus*, 1820 (pl. XXV)

Revett, Nicholas *see* Stuart, James and Revett, Nicholas
Rottiers, Bernard, *Description des monumens de Rhodes*, Brussels, 1830
Scenes in Athens; Drawn and Tinted by Mary Hogarth, Described by David Hogarth, London and New York, 190[?]
Scrofani, Saverio, *Viaggio in Grecia*, 2 vols, London, 1799
Smirke, Robert, diary. Royal Institute of British Architects, London, MS CC12
Spratt, Captain, T. A. B., *Travels and Researches in Crete*, 2 vols, London, 1865
Stackelberg, Otto Magnus von, *Trachten und Gebräuche der Neugriechen*, Berlin, 1831
La Grèce. Vues pittoresques et topographiques, Paris, 1834
Stademann, Ferdinand, *Panorama von Athen*, Munich, 1841
Stuart, James and Revett, Nicholas, *The Antiquities of Athens Measured and Delineated*, 4 vols, London, 1762–1816
Symonds, John Addington, *Sketches and Studies in Italy and Greece*, Third Series, new edition, London, 1898
Townshend, Frederick Trench, *A Cruise in Greek Waters*, London, 1870
Travlos, John, *Neoclassical Architecture in Greece* (in Greek), Athens, 1967
Turner, William, *Journal of a Tour in the Levant*, 3 vols, London, 1820
Waddington, George, *A Visit to Greece in 1823 and 1824*, London, 1825
Williams, Hugh William, *Travels in Italy, Greece and the Ionian Islands*, 2 vols, Edinburgh 1820
Wilson, The Rev. Samuel Sheridan, *A Narrative of the Greek Mission; or Sixteen Years in Malta and Greece*, London, 1839
Wordsworth, Christopher, *Greece: Pictorial, Descriptive and Historical*, London, 1839

Annotated catalogue of the illustrations

PART I

p. 2 (*frontispiece*) Louis Dupré, *The House of the French Consul in Athens*, 1819
From L. Dupré, *Voyage à Athènes et Constantinople*, Paris, 1825, pl. 19
Coloured lithograph, 33.5 × 40 cm

The house of Louis Sébastien Fauvel, the French consul at Athens, was situated in the centre of the ancient Agora. A great number of marble fragments and plaster casts of statues were exhibited in the inner courtyard of the house. The house was destroyed during the Greek Revolution.

Louis Dupré (1789–1837) visited Greece in 1819. He exhibited Greek subjects at the Salons of 1827, 1831, 1833 and 1855. In 1825 he published a set of coloured lithographs of views and studies of costumes from Greece, entitled *Voyage à Athènes et Constantinople*.

p. 10 Giovanni Battista Lusieri, *The Monument of Philopappus*, 1800
Watercolour
The Earl of Elgin and Kincardie collection

The Monument of Philopappus which stands on the Museum Hill, was built between AD 114 and 116 in honour of Gaius Julius Antiochos Philopappus, a Syrian, citizen of Athens and benefactor of the city.

Giovanni Battista Lusieri (1751–1821) was Court Painter to the King of Naples when recruited by William R. Hamilton for Elgin's expedition. He was referred to by travellers as 'Don Tita'. He remained in Athens until all the marbles had been shipped to London.
BIBLIOGRAPHY: H. W. Williams, *Travels in Italy, Greece and the Ionian Islands*, Edinburgh, 1820, pp. 330–3; A. H. Smith, 'Lord Elgin and his Collection', in *Journal of Hellenic Studies*, XXXVI (1916), pp. 173–5; W. St Clair, *Lord Elgin and the Marbles*, London, 1967, pp. 30–1.

p. 12 *Map of Greece*
From Ptolemy's *Geographia*, Bologna, 1477
Woodcut, 35 × 40 cm

The cartography of the age of the great discoveries was based upon two types of maps: the portulans (*portolano*), and the so-called Ptolemaic maps. The latter were based upon the descriptions of the Alexandrian geographer Claudius Ptolemaeus (active *c*. AD 150). In his work γεωγραφική ὑφήγησις he presented the most detailed description of ἡ οἰκουμένη, or the whole world as it was then known to the Greeks, giving systematic instructions for cartography. Manuscript maps, drawn according to Ptolemy's descriptions, were copied by the Byzantines and later spread to the West by way of the Byzantine scholars who fled to Italy after the fall of Constantinople. The first edition of Ptolemy's *Geographia*, or *Cosmographia*, as the work became known, appeared in Bologna in 1477. This edition included the earliest separate maps of the Hellenic world. Increasingly, in the thirteenth century, the coast of Greece and the islands of the archipelago, because of their strategic position on one of the most important maritime and commercial highways of the then known world, were frequented by Genoese, Venetian and Neapolitan merchants. During the Renaissance famous cartographers, such as Johannes Laurenberg (1527–1658), Gerardus Mercator (1512–94), Sebastian Munster (1489–1552) and Abraham Ortelius (1527–98), attempted to produce more accurate depictions of the coasts and islands of the Mediterranean to meet the needs of the growing numbers of Dutch, French and English navigators. In the oldest maps of Greece, cities were indicated by their ancient names. Gradually, separate types of map for ancient and modern Greece were created, bearing the titles *Graecia antiqua*, and *Nova Graecia* or *European Turkey*. In some cases the same map had both titles, together with the Latin inscription *olim-nunc* (formerly-nowadays).
BIBLIOGRAPHY: L. Bagrow and R. A. Skelton, *History of Cartography*, London, 1964; R. V. Tooley, *Maps and Mapmakers*, 6th ed., London, 1978; D. Flambouras, 'The First Printed Portulans of the Greek Islands' (in Greek), in *Zygos*, 9 (July–August 1974), pp. 26–37; C. Zacharakis, *A Printed Survey of Greece* (in Greek), Nicosia, 1976.

p. 13 *View of Chios*
From George Braun and Franz Hogenberg, *Civitates Orbis Terrarum*, 6 vols, Cologne, 1572–1618
Woodcut, 31 × 45.5 cm

Very little is known of the creators of the ambitious, six-volume *Civitates Orbis Terrarum*. Georg Braun (1541–1622) was a priest from Cologne, and Franz Hogenberg (1535–90) a Flemish engraver. The work's originality derived from the fact that it was an atlas devoted exclusively to views of cities. Clearly depicted in this view of Chios are the famous mastic trees on the mountains, the main product and source of wealth of the island.
BIBLIOGRAPHY: A. Hibbert and R. Oehme, *Old European Cities: Twenty-four 16th-century City Maps and Texts from the 'Civitates Orbis Terrarum' of Georg Braun and Franz Hogenberg*, London, 1955.

p. 14 *An Orthodox Priest*
From André Thevet, *Cosmographie de Levant*, Lyon, 1554
Woodcut, 12 × 10 cm

The French geographer-priest André Thevet (1502–90) is known for his world-map in the shape of the fleur-de-lys and for his accurate maps of the four continents. Thevet travelled widely in Greece between 1549 and 1555. On his return to France he was appointed Royal Historiographer and Geographer. His *Cosmographie* is the most complete geography of the sixteenth-century Greek world.

Michael Wolgemuth, *View of Setines (Athens)*
From Hartmann Schedel, *Liber Chronicarum*, Nürnberg, 1493
Woodcut, 14 × 22 cm

The *Liber Chronicarum*, or *Nuremberg Chronicle*, was the most lavishly illustrated book of the fifteenth century. It was a sort of encyclopaedia in which the author attempted to synthesize all the mythological and historical knowledge of his time. The two thousand woodcuts in the book were executed by Michael Wolgemuth (1434–1519) and Wilhelm Pleydenwurff (d. 1494), whose studio was the most famous of the period. Albrecht Dürer is reputed to have worked there for three years (1486–9) and it is therefore probable that he participated in the project, although it should be remembered that he was then only a fifteen-year-old apprentice. There are altogether eight illustrations of Greek cities in the book – Athens, Corinth, Candia (Crete), Rhodes, Lacedaemon, Achaea, Thrace and Macedonia – although the same images are repeated elsewhere with different titles as other cities of Europe. Only two are authentic: *Candia*, and *Rhodes*, where the artist copied the plates from another famous book of the period, Bernhard von Breydenbach's *Peregrinationes in Terram Sanctam*, Mainz, 1486 (with illustrations by Erhard Reuwich). The other views are imaginary in rendering and subject, symptomatic of the lack of knowledge about Greece at this time (Achaea, Macedonia and Thrace, for example, were never cities).

BIBLIOGRAPHY: E. Rüker, *Die Schedelsche Weltchronik*, Munich, 1973; E. Panofsky, *The Life and Art of Albrecht Dürer*, Princeton, N.J., 1955; D. Flamouras, 'The Chronicle of Hartmann Schedel' (in Greek), in *Zygos*, 15–17 (July–December 1975), pp. 42–53.

p. 15 Jacques Carrey, *The West and East Pediments of the Parthenon*, 1674
From the Comte de la Borde, *Athènes aux XVe, XVIe et XVII siècles*, 2 vols, Paris, 1854

Jacques Carrey (1649–1726) was a pupil in the studio of Charles Lebrun when Lebrun was asked by the Marquis de Nointel to recommend a competent artist to accompany him on an expedition to the Aegean Islands and Asia Minor.

Carrey executed a large number of drawings during the course of the expedition, the most important of which are a series of drawings of the Parthenon. These are, in fact, unique, since, as a fortress, the Acropolis was forbidden to foreigners.

Nointel, in his capacity as special ambassador, obtained permission for his artist to record the ancient buildings. Throughout the month of December 1674 Carrey, under the supervision of a janissary, made drawings of the Parthenon frieze and pediments. His drawings are the only records of the almost perfectly surviving sculptures of the pediments which, a few years later, were to be largely destroyed by Morosini. On Carrey's return to France, the drawings were lost, but they were rediscovered in 1797. In 1811 they were published in a luxurious volume entitled *Temple de Minerve à Athènes* under Carrey's name. In 1848 the Comte de la Borde underwrote a facsimile edition entitled *Le Parthenon, documents pour servir à une restauration*. Carrey's drawings are now deposited in the Bibliothèque Nationale, Paris.

BIBLIOGRAPHY: A. Vendal, *L'Odyssée d'un ambassadeur 1670–80*, Paris, 1900; Henri Omont, *Athènes au XVIIe siècle*, Paris, 1896; H. Viardot, 'De la destruction des oeuvres d'art', in *Gazette des Beaux Arts* (1874), pp. 392–400; The Comte de la Borde, *Athènes aux XVe, XVIe et XVIIe siècles*, 2 vols, Paris, 1854; Lya and Raymond Matton, *Athènes et ses monuments: du XVIIe siècle à nos jours*, Athens, 1963.

p. 16 Vicenzo Maria Coronelli, *The Siege of Kalamata by the Venetian Army*
From V. M. Coronelli, *Morea*, Venice, 1685–6

Engraving, 30 × 40 cm
The Franciscan monk Vicenzo Maria Coronelli (1650–1718) was the official Cosmographer of the Venetian Republic. In 1680 he founded the first Cartographic Society, or Academia Cosmografia degli Argonauti. In 1684, during the Veneto–Turkish War, he published his *Conquiste della Republica in Dalmazi, Epiro e Morea* and *Memorie istoriografiche delli regni della Morea, e Negroponte*, subsequently republished in 1685–6 as the two-volume *Morea*. In 1701 he published his *Mediterraneo*. Coronelli's works are of considerable importance for the subsequent development of Greek topography.

BIBLIOGRAPHY: Ermanno Armao, *In giro per il Mar Egeo con V. Coronelli*, Venice, 1951; P. Kilimis, 'The Geographical Work of V. Coronelli with Special Reference to Greece' (in Greek), in *Bulletin of the Greek Geographical Society*, Athens, 1952.

p. 17 *The Bombardment of the Parthenon by the Venetian Army on 26 September 1687*
After the original drawing made on the spot by Giacomo Milheau Verneda
Engraving, 25 × 72.5 cm

Giacomo Milheau Verneda was an artillery officer in the Venetian army and was present at the siege of the Acropolis in 1687. It seems that he was requested to make a drawing of the bombardment by Admiral Francesco Morosini. Verneda's original drawing is now in the Frari Archives in Venice.

BIBLIOGRAPHY: Henri Omont, *Athènes au XVIIe siècle*, Paris, 1896.

View of Misithra (Mistras)
From Bernard Randolph, *The Present State of the Morea*, Oxford, 1685
Engraving, 15.5 × 21.5 cm

Bernard Randolph (1643–90) undertook a tour of the Peloponnesus and the Greek islands in 1671–9. His description of the islands appeared in his *The Present State of the Islands in the Archipelago*, published in 1687, which also includes an original map of Greece with a view of Constantinople.

p. 18 Jacob Spon, *The Tower of the Winds* and *The Lysicrates Monument*
From J. Spon, *Voyage d'Italie, de Dalmatie, de Grèce et du Levant*, Lyon, 1678
Engraving, 17 × 13 cm

The French doctor Jacob Spon (1647–85) and the English naturalist George Wheler (1650–1723) met in Venice in 1675, and began their eight-month tour of Greece and Asia Minor the same year. They spent a month in Athens studying its classical monuments, which are depicted, with detailed descriptions of their contemporary condition, in Spon's book. Four years later, Wheler published his account of the tour, accompanied with yet less accurate illustrations.

BIBLIOGRAPHY: The Comte de la Borde, *Athènes au XVe, XVIe et XVIIe siècles*, Paris, 1854, vol. II, pp. 1–54.

p. 19 Julien David Le Roy, *An Imaginary Greek Landscape*
From J. D. Le Roy, *Ruins of Athens with Remains and Other Valuable Antiquities in Greece*, London, 1759 (printed for R. Sayer)
Engraving, 29 × 40 cm

The French architect Julien David Le Roy (1728–1803) visited Greece in 1755–6. The first edition of his *Les Ruines . . .* was published in 1758.

p. 22 J. K. Ch. J. Haller von Hallerstein, *View of the Theseum*, 1810
Watercolour, 34 × 52 cm
Bibliothèque Nationale et Universitaire de Strasbourg

Johann Karl Christoph J. Haller von Hallerstein (1774–1817), the favourite architect of Crown Prince Ludwig of Bavaria, was sent to Greece in 1810–11, where he took part in the excavations at Aegina and at Bassae. He remained in Greece until his death in 1817. Today the largest collection of his drawings is in the Bibliothèque Nationale et Universitaire de Strasbourg. Unfortunately, all his Greek drawings, with the exception of those of Bassae, were lost in a shipwreck in December 1812.

BIBLIOGRAPHY: Georges Roux, *Karl Haller von Hallerstein, Le Temple de Bassae*, Strasbourg, 1976; H. W. Williams, *Travels in Italy, Greece and the Ionian Islands*, Edinburgh, 1820, vol. II, pp. 33–4 (for a contemporary estimate of Hallerstein's work).

p. 23 Charles Robert Cockerell, *Excavations at the Temple of Aphaea in Aegina*, 1811
From C. R. Cockerell, *The Temples of Jupiter Panhellenius at Aegina, and of Apollo Epicurius at Bassae near Phigaleia in Arcadia*, London, 1860, pl. II
Engraving, 24 × 36 cm

Cockerell describes the excavations thus:
'As it was our intention to examine thoroughly this curious edifice, we pitched our tent under a rock and took possession of a cave close by, which made an excellent dwelling for our servants and janizzary. In the execution of our object we set three men to dig and turn over stones or blocks whose measurement might conduce to the purposes of elucidation: on the second morning as we were removing rubbish from the interior of the portico, we turned up two heads of Parian marble, perfectly entire in all their features: after these a beautiful leg and foot

appeared, and not to tire you with a circumstantial detail of our progress, we discovered under the two fronts of the temple (which faced E. and W.) sixteen figures and thirteen heads, legs, arms, &c. all in the highest state of preservation ... You may easily imagine that during the progress of this extraordinary discovery we were not a little surprised at our good fortune, and that among so many travellers who have visited this famous temple during so many centuries we should be the first with curiosity enough to dig three feet deep' (The Rev. Thomas Smart Hughes, *Travels in Sicily, Greece and Albania*, London, 1820, vol. I, p. 283).

Charles Robert Cockerell (1788–1863) visited Greece in 1810–11 and again in 1812–13. In 1830 and 1831 he exhibited at the Royal Academy a set of drawings depicting his imaginary restoration of the Parthenon. The majority of his Greek drawings are now in the British Museum and the Royal Institute of British Architects, London.

Cockerell published the following works on Greece: *Antiquities of Athens, and Other Places in Greece, Sicily, etc. supplementary to the Antiquities of Athens by J. Stuart and N. Revett*, London, 1830; *The Temples of Jupiter Panhellenius at Aegina, and of Apollo Epicurius at Bassae near Phigaleia in Arcadia*, London, 1860.

BIBLIOGRAPHY: S. P. Cockerell, *Travels in Southern Europe and the Levant, 1810–17. The Journal of C. R. Cockerell, R.A.*, London, 1903, and 'The Life and Works of C. R. Cockerell, R.A.', in *Architectural Review*, 12 (1902), pp. 43–7; D. Watkin, *The Life and Work of C. R. Cockerell*, London, 1974.

p. 24 Benjamin Robert Haydon, *Torso of Dionysus Exhibited in the Park Lane Museum*, 1809
Pencil drawing, 44.5 × 62 cm
The Earl of Elgin and Kincardine collection

'To Park Lane then we went, and after passing through the hall and thence into an open yard, entered a damp, dirty pent-house where lay the marbles ranged within sight and reach ... That combination of nature and idea, which I had felt was so much wanting for high art, was here displayed to midday conviction. My heart beat! If I had seen nothing else I had beheld sufficient to keep me to nature for the rest of my life ... Here were principles which the common sense of the English people would understand; ... here were the principles which the great Greeks in their finest time established, and here was I, the most prominent historical student, perfectly qualified to appreciate all this ... I felt as if a divine

truth had blazed inwardly upon my mind and I knew that they would at last rouse the art of Europe from its slumber in the darkness' (B. R. Haydon, *Autobiography and Memoirs*, ed. Aldous Huxley, London, 1926, p. 66).

Although Benjamin Robert Haydon (1786–1846) never visited Greece, he was the most enthusiastic champion of the Elgin Marbles and made a thorough study of them during 1808–13. There are extensive collections of his drawings of the Elgin Marbles in the British Museum and the Royal Academy, London.

BIBLIOGRAPHY: W. B. Pope (ed.), *The Diary of Benjamin Robert Haydon*, 5 vols, Cambridge, Mass., 1960–3; Eric George, *The Life and Death of Benjamin Robert Haydon*, Oxford, 1967; F. Cummings, 'Phidias in Bloomsbury: B. R. Haydon's Drawings of the Elgin Marbles', in *Burlington Magazine*, CVI (1964), pp. 323–8.

p. 25 Charles Robert Cockerell, *Lord Elgin's Museum at Park Lane*, 1808
Pencil drawing, 30 × 35 cm
British Museum, London

The Elgin Marbles were first exhibited in a temporary museum in Park Lane in 1807. In 1812, when the second shipment arrived in England, the whole collection was removed to the forecourt of Burlington House.

p. 27 Antoine Laurent Castellan, *A Greek Shepherd*
From A. L. Castellan, *Lettres sur la Morée*, Paris, 1808, pl. 9
Engraving, 9 × 14.5 cm

In the text accompanying the engraving Castellan wrote: 'The Shepherds [in the Morea] are such as are depicted in the *Idylls* by Theocritus or as are represented in the Greek reliefs.'

Antoine Laurent Castellan (1772–1838) made a brief tour of Greece in 1796 as a member of the French expedition of military engineers who were engaged in repairing and fortifying the port at Constantinople.

Castellan published the following works on Greece: *Lettres sur la Morée et les îles de Cerigo, Hydra et Zante*, 1808; *Lettres sur la Grèce, l'Hellespont et Constantinople, faisant suite aux lettres sur la Morée*, Paris, 1811.

BIBLIOGRAPHY: A. Boppe, *Les Peintres du Bosphore au 18e siècle*, Paris, 1911, pp. 210–12.

p. 31 William Gell, *A View of Athens 'à la Poussin'*, 1800
Sepia drawing, 21.5 × 35 cm
Benaki Museum, Athens

The following description by Gell appears on the verso:
'The view is that of Athens from the

sacred way to Eleusis. On the left of the town is Mt. Anchesmus, the rocks on its summit are red and yellow. On the right of the city is the Acropolis & Temple of Minerva which is white marble with a yellowish tint here & there. Right of that is the hill of the Museum with a white marble monument on its summit. The hill under the Temple of Minerva with a tower upon is that of the Areopagus & is separated by a narrow valley from the hill of the citadel and the nearer hill which I have shaded a little.'

Sir William Gell (1777–1836) visited Greece in 1804 and 1806. The majority of his Greek works are now in the British Museum, London, but there is a sketchbook from his 1804 Greek tour in the Benaki Museum, Athens.

Gell published the following illustrated works on Greece: *The Geography and Antiquities of Ithaca*, London, 1807; *Itinerary of the Morea*, London, 1817; *The Itinerary of Greece; Containing One Hundred Routes in Attica, Boeotia ... and Thessaly*, London, 1819; *Narrative of a Journey in the Morea*, London, 1823.

Colour Plates I–VII (pp. 32–41)

I Eugène Delacroix, *A Greek Warrior*, c. 1820
Ink and watercolour, 29.2 × 22.7 cm
Signed with initials
Stavros Niarchos collection

Eugène Delacroix (1798–1863) may be considered the Philhellenic artist *par excellence*, producing numerous works on Greek subjects from the outbreak of the Revolution in 1820 until the year before his death. His first major Greek work, *The Massacre of Scio*, was exhibited at the Salon in 1824 and undoubtedly moved even the hearts of those who were indifferent to the Greek cause. In 1826 he sent four paintings to the Galerie Lebrun in aid of the Greeks (see *Revue encyclopédique*, XXX (1826), pp. 578–80), probably including his *Greece Expiring on the Ruins of Missolonghi*, which was exhibited at the Salon the following year. It was this masterpiece, more than any other contemporary painting, which came to symbolize the distress of Philhellenic Europe for the pathetic situation of the Greeks.

BIBLIOGRAPHY: René Huyghe, *Delacroix*, London, 1963, and *Delacroix and Greece*, Athens, 1971.

II James Stuart, *Stuart Sketching the Erechtheum*, 1751
Watercolour, 26.5 × 38.5 cm
Royal Institute of British Architects, London

The view is engraved with slight alterations in Stuart and Revett's *Antiquities of Athens*, vol. II (1787), ch. II, pl. II.

James Stuart (1713–88) met Nicholas Revett in Rome. In 1748 the two men issued *Proposals for Publishing an Accurate Description of the Antiquities of Athens*. The scheme attracted the attention of the English Society of Dilettanti and with assistance from a number of members of the Society they were enabled to go to Athens where they stayed from March 1751 until the autumn of 1753. Stuart made all the general drawings for the *Antiquities* and Revett supplied all the measurements. They returned to England in 1755, after having visited the islands of the Archipelago. Although it was Revett who was responsible for all the measured drawings that gave the *Antiquities* its unique importance, it was Stuart who was made famous by its publication, and who was henceforward known as 'Athenian' Stuart.

BIBLIOGRAPHY: James Stuart and Nicholas Revett, *The Antiquities of Athens Measured and Delineated*, 4 vols, London, 1762–1816; Lesley Lawrence, 'Stuart and Revett: Their Literary and Architectural Careers', in *Journal of the Warburg and Courtauld Institutes*, 2 (1938), pp. 128–46; D. Wiebenson, *Sources of Greek Revival Architecture*, London, 1969; J. Mordaunt Crook, *The Greek Revival*, London, 1972.

III Louis François Cassas, *Hadrian's Aqueduct*, 1775
Watercolour, 46 × 65 cm
Museum of the City of Athens

Louis François Cassas (1756–1827) visited Greece in about 1775. A series of aquatints based on his Greek views was published in 1813 entitled:
Grandes vues pittoresques des principaux sites et monumens de la Grèce et de la Sicile et des Sept Collines de Rome. Dessinées et gravées . . . par MM. Cassas et Bence.
BIBLIOGRAPHY: *Revue encyclopédique*, 37 (1828), pp. 317–18; A. Boppe, *Les Peintres du Bosphore au 18e siècle*, Paris, 1911, pp. 151–3, 209–10.

IV Charles Lock Eastlake, *Byron's 'Dream'*, 1829
Oil on canvas, 114 × 167 cm
Exhibited at the Royal Academy, London, in 1829 (157)
Tate Gallery, London

The Doric temple on the right can be identified as the temple of Sunium, and the colonnade on the far left as the Gate of the Agora in Athens. Eastlake painted the mountains in the background from a sketch he had made in Naples in March 1824: 'The mountains on the eastern side of the bay are exactly what I want

for my Greek landscape (Byron's Dream),' he had written then (*Contributions to the Literature of the Fine Arts, 2nd Series*, with a memoir by Lady Eastlake, London, 1870, p. 105). The painting seems to be based on Turner's *View of the Temple of Jupiter Panhellenius, in the Island of Aegina, with the Greek National Dance of the Romaika: the Acropolis of Athens in the Distance*, exhibited at the Royal Academy in 1816. The composition is heavily framed on the left by a group of trees, and the Temple of Jupiter is seen within an area of light, but Turner's central mass of wooded hills and trees has been replaced by lofty cypresses. Nevertheless, Eastlake has achieved a remarkable unity of effect and colour: the bright sky, dark blue sea and rusty surface of the columns are successfully rendered, and the clear atmosphere faithfully revealed.

Sir Charles Lock Eastlake (1793–1865) visited Greece in 1819 on a commission from his patron, Jeremiah Harman, to make sketches of the scenery. A list of Greek works painted by him in 1820–21, 1826–9, 1833 and 1837 is given in Lady Eastlake's *Memoir* (see Bibliography). A series of his watercolour sketches of Greek costumes is in a private collection, London.

BIBLIOGRAPHY: Lady Eastlake, *A Memoir of Sir Charles Lock Eastlake*, London, 1869; *Sir Charles Lock Eastlake, P.R.A. 1793–1865*, exhibition catalogue, City Art Gallery, Plymouth, 1965; F. M. Tsigakou, 'Edward Lear in Greece', unpublished M. Phil. thesis, University College, London, 1977, pp. 55–8; David Robertson, *Sir Charles Lock Eastlake and the Victorian Art World*, Princeton, N.J., 1977.

V E. F. Green, *Landscape with a Greek Girl*, 1835
Oil on canvas, 61.5 × 48.5 cm
Signed and dated
Private collection, Athens

Very little is known about E. F. Green, who was active during the first half of the nineteenth century. He exhibited a series of works of Greek subjects at the British Institution and the Society of British Artists in 1834 and 1835.

VI Christian Perlberg, *Fête by the Olympieum*, 1838
Oil on canvas, 51.5 × 59.5 cm
National Historical Museum, Athens

Christian Johann Georg Perlberg (1806–84), a painter of genre scenes, went to Greece in 1834
BIBLIOGRAPHY: Johann Jacob Merlo, *Kölnische Künstler in alter und neuer Zeit*, Düsseldorf, 1895, pp. 663 ff.

VII Joseph Mallord William Turner, *'T'is living Greece no more'*, 1822

Watercolour, 39 × 28 cm
Signed and dated
Museum of the City of Athens

Turner never actually visited Greece, although he nearly did so early in his career when he was approached by Lord Elgin in 1799 to act as his draughtsman on the expedition to Athens that he was planning. It is typical that financial considerations should have been the reason for Turner refusing the offer. As Lord Elgin later told the Select Committee of the House of Commons, which considered the purchase of his collection: 'I applied to such artists here as were recommended to me as likely to answer the purpose, in particular to Mr Turner, to go upon my account. Mr Turner's objection to my plan was, that as the object was of a general nature, and that the condition I insisted upon was, that the whole results of all the artists should be collected together and left with me; he objected, because he wished to retain a portion of his own labour for his own use; he moreover asked between seven and eight hundred pounds of salary, independently of his expenses being paid, which of course was out of my reach altogether' (see A. H. Smith, 'Lord Elgin and his Collection', in *Journal of Hellenic Studies*, XXXVI (1916), p. 166).

Nevertheless, Turner executed a number of Greek subjects, in which he made use of the sketches of other artists. *View of the Temple of Jupiter Penhellenius, in the Island of Aegina, with the Greek National Dance of the Romaika: the Acropolis of Athens in the Distance* (oil on canvas, 182 × 178 cm) was the only picture by Turner of a subject set in Greece to be exhibited at the Royal Academy (1816). Turner's later Greek subjects were closely related to the contemporary literary vogue for Byron's *Childe Harold*. Although it has been supposed that the use of Byronic themes in Turner's work came after the exhibition of Eastlake's *Byron's 'Dream'*, specifically during the early 1830s (see John Gage, 'Turner's Academic Friendships: C. L. Eastlake', in *Burlington Magazine*, CX (1968), pp. 667–85), he had in fact contributed illustrations to Byron's poems in 1825. Altogether Turner made twenty-six drawings for three different editions of Byron's works, published between 1825 and 1834: *Lord Byron's Works*, 11 vols (with seven engravings by Turner), London, John Murray, 1825; *The Works of Lord Byron: with his Letters and Journals and his Life, by Thomas More*, 17 vols (with seventeen vignettes by Turner), London, John Murray, 1832–4; *Finden's Landscape and Portrait Illustrations of the Life and Works of Lord Byron*, 3 vols (with the seven engravings of the 1825 edition together with two new plates),

London, John Murray and Charles Tilt, 1833–4.

p. 42 J. L. David, after a drawing by Antoine de Favray, *A Greek Funeral*
From Pierre Augustin Guys, *Voyage littéraire de la Grèce, ou lettres sur les Grecs anciens et modernes*, 2 vols, Paris, 1776
Engraving, 16 × 20 cm

The French painter Antoine de Favray (1706–98) held the title of Knight of the Order of Malta. He spent many years in that island. Between 1762 and 1771 he was established in Constantinople, as the painter of the French ambassador. It was in Constantinople that he met Guys and was asked by him to make a series of portraits of the ladies of the Phanariot families living in Constantinople. Favray's Greek works are illustrated in the second edition of Guys's *Voyage*, published in 1776 (see also the revised edition of 1783).
BIBLIOGRAPHY: A. Boppe, *Les Peintres du Bosphore au 18e siècle*, Paris, 1911, pp. 57–100.

p. 43 *Greece Expiring among Classical Ruins*, 1782
From the Comte de Choiseul-Gouffier, *Voyage pittoresque de la Grèce*, 3 vols, Paris, 1782–1802, vol. I (1782), frontispiece
Engraving, 20 × 20 cm

The Comte de Choiseul-Gouffier (1752–1817) first visited Greece in 1776 as a member of the French Scientific Expedition to the Mediterranean. Twenty years later he was appointed French ambassador to Constantinople where he remained until 1793.
For a concise bibliography, see A. Koumarianou, 'Choiseul-Gouffier's Travels' (in Greek), in L. Droulia *et al*, *Travels in Greece*, Athens, 1968, pp. 46–8.

p. 44 Louis Dupré, *A Klepht*
From F. C. H. L. Pouqueville, *Voyage dans la Grèce ... avec cartes, vues et figures*, 6 vols, Paris, 1826–7, vol. I, frontispiece

The frontispiece from vol. I of the second edition of Pouqueville's *Voyage de la Grèce*, first published in 1820–1.
The French doctor François Charles Henri Pouqueville was a member of Napoleon's expedition to Egypt. During the voyage back to France, in 1799, his ship was captured by pirates. But when the latter put in to the shores of the Morea for provisions, all the French captives were taken prisoner by the Turks, because of the outbreak of the Franco–Turkish War. Pouqueville spent seven months in Tripolitza and was then sent to Constantinople, where he spent another year in prison. On his return to France he published an account of his adventures which he dedicated to Napoleon, entitled *Voyage en Morée, à Constantinople, en Albanie et dans plusiers autres parties de l'Empire othoman* (Paris, 1805). Despite the fact that Pouqueville had only visited some of the places he describes, the book was so successful that it was translated into most of the European languages. Moreover it gained for Pouqueville the apointment as Napoleon's consul at Ioannina, where he stayed for ten years from 1806 to 1816. During this time he had an opportunity to travel extensively in Greece and to compose a more reliable account of the country, which appeared as *Voyage dans la Grèce* in 1820, on the eve of the Revolution.

p. 45 Ferdinand Bauer, *Vignette with a View of Parnassus*, 1806
From *Flora Graeca*, vol. I, London, 1806, frontispiece
Coloured lithograph, 34 × 21 cm

The English botanist John Sibthorp (1758–96) made an extensive tour in Greece in 1786–7, and again in 1794–5. On his first tour he was accompanied by the Austrian artist Ferdinand Bauer (1760–1826) who made watercolour drawings of botanical specimens throughout the country. Sibthorp died soon after his return to England from his second tour. His observations on Greek plants with illustrations by Bauer were published between 1806 and 1840 in ten lavishly illustrated volumes entitled *Flora Graeca*.

p. 47 H. L. V. J. B. Aubry–Lecomte, *Chateaubriand and Mme de Staël among the Greeks*, 1827
After the original painting by F. P. S. Gérard, *Corinne au Cap de Misène*
Lithograph, 25.5 × 29.5 cm

The original painting by F. P. S. Baron de Gérard was bought by Mme Récamier. The lithograph was exhibited in the Salon of 1827 and was highly acclaimed: 'Une des plus remarquables qui soient sorties des presses lithographiques de France,' wrote the *Courrier français* (7 December 1827) (see also *Revue encyclopédique*, 35 (1827), p. 819). The original painting was extraordinarily popular in France; versions of the composition occur frequently on glassware and porcelain. In addition, the figure of Chateaubriand was widely reproduced in lithographs. But the most widely circulated of all was the figure of the young man on the left: many lithographic versions of his portrait appeared with the title 'Le jeune Grec'.
The Neoclassical painter François Pascal Simon, Baron Gérard (1770–1837) never visited Greece. H. L. V. J. B.

Aubry-Lecomte (1787–1858) was one of the most eminent French lithographers of the early nineteenth century.

p. 50 Eugène Delacroix, *A Mounted Greek Warrior*, 1856
Oil on canvas, 65.5 × 81 cm
National Gallery, Athens

Delacroix treated a similar subject in a painting exhibited under the title *An Episode from the Current War between the Greeks and the Turks* at the Salon of 1827 (see René Huyghe, *Delacroix and Greece*, Athens, 1971).

p. 51 Louis Dupré, *Landscape with a Greek*, c. 1830
Oil on canvas, 51.5 × 36 cm
Benaki Museum, Athens

The picture is similar in style, setting and pose to that entitled 'Un Grec de Janina' in Dupré's *Voyage à Athènes et Constantinople*, 1825, pl. X.

Antoine Charles Horace Vernet, *The Defeat*, 1827
Oil on canvas, 44 × 34 cm
Signed and dated
Benaki Museum, Athens

For a criticism of the painting, see *Annales de l'Ecole française des Beaux Arts*, (1827), pp. 67–9. According to contemporary descriptions the picture shows a Greek standing over a dead Turk, asking the Turk's servant to take his master's head with his own sword.
Antoine Charles Horace Vernet (1758–1836), known as 'Carle' Vernet, never visited Greece. He contributed Greek works to the Salon of 1828 and to the exhibition 'au profit des Grecs' at the Galerie Lebrun, in 1826. There is a painting by him, *A Scene from the Greek War of Independence*, in the Archbishop's Palace, Nicosia, Cyprus.

Richard Parkes Bonington, *Portrait of a Young Greek*, c. 1825–6
Oil on canvas, 35.5 × 27.5 cm
Benaki Museum, Athens

The picture resembles Delacroix's *Count Palatiano* (1826) and was, in fact, formerly attributed to Delacroix.
Richard Parkes Bonington (1801–28) never visited Greece, but a member of the Delacroix circle, a certain Monsieur Auguste, had travelled extensively in the East, and had brought back many costumes. Delacroix made use of them when he was working on the *Massacre of Scio*, and Bonington could well have made drawings of a model wearing Greek costume at the same time.

p. 52 Karl Krazeisen, *Greeks Fighting among Classical Ruins*, 1829
Oil on canvas, 28.5 × 22 cm
Mike Krassakis collection, Cologne

The same composition appears as a lithograph in Krazeisen's *Bildnisse ausgezeichneter Griechen und Philhellenen nebst einigen Ansichten und Trachten*, Munich, 1828–31, pl. III.

Karl Krazeisen (1794–1878) was in Greece in 1826–7 as a subaltern in the Philhellenic Regiment under the command of Karl von Heydeck. The majority of the drawings he made in Greece are now in the National Gallery, Athens. BIBLIOGRAPHY: *Warriors of 1821: Twenty Pencil Drawings by Karl Krazeisen* (in Greek), exhibition catalogue organized by the Fine Art School, Athens, 1971.

Bronze ink-stand with statuette of Markos Botsaris dying
French, *c.* 1835–40
H. 10.5 cm
Based on a sculpture by David d'Angers, *A Young Girl Stooping and Deciphering on a Tombstone the Name of Botsaris*, now in the National Gallery, Athens.

Louis Dupré, *The Virgin of Thyamis*
From L. Dupré, *Voyage à Athènes et Constantinople*, Paris, 1825
Lithograph, 21.5 × 21.5 cm

Thyamis is the name of a river in Epirus.

p. 53 Joseph Denis Odevaere, *The Death of Byron*, 1826
Oil on canvas, 166 × 234.5 cm
Signed
Groeninge Museum, Bruges

The composition is reminiscent of David's *Death of Marat* (1793). The inscriptions on the medallions which decorate the bed are titles of Byron's poems. The poet's hand lies on a lyre with its strings broken. The antique sculpture above, against which the poet's sword is resting, is inscribed in Greek 'Eleutheria' (Liberty).

The Belgian artist Joseph Denis Odevaere (1775–1830) worked for a short period under David in Paris in the late 1780s. Another picture of a Greek subject by him is *The Last Defenders of Missolonghi*, dated 1826, in the Rijksmuseum, Amsterdam.

p. 54 Lodovico Lipparini, *Byron's Oath at Missolonghi*, 1824
Oil on panel, 17 × 22 cm
Benaki Museum, Athens

Byron is depicted swearing an oath upon the grave of Botsaris at Missolonghi. The Suliote family of the Botsaris presented a long list of famous names in the Greek War of Independence. Markos (1790–1823) was the most heroic. After the fall of Suli in July 1822, he joined the Greek military forces at Missolonghi and was named

General. He was killed in battle on 9 August 1823 and was buried at Missolonghi.

Another version of this subject is in the Museo Civico, Treviso. Lodovico Lipparini (1800–56) painted a series of works inspired by the Greek Revolution, including *Death of a Suliote* (1839), *A Greek who Contemplates on the Fate of his Country, Botsaris's Farewell, The Death of Markos Botsaris, The Flight from Parga* and *The Oath of the Greeks to Archbishop Germanos* (for Lipparini's historical subjects, see P. Barrocchi *et al.*, *Romanticismo storico*, Florence, 1974, pp. 175, 306 ff.).

Ary Scheffer, *A Young Greek Defending his Wounded Father*, 1827
Oil on canvas, 45 × 37 cm
Benaki Museum, Athens

There is a tapestry of the same subject in a private collection in Athens (see illustration on p. 66 above). Although Scheffer never visited Greece, he painted a series of works inspired by the Greek Revolution between 1825 and 1830, including the following: *The Last Defenders of Missolonghi in the Moment of Setting Fire to the Gunpowder that Will Cause their Death; Young Greek Girls Imploring the Virgin's Protection during a Battle; Suliote Women*.
BIBLIOGRAPHY: *Ary Scheffer 1795–1858*, exhibition catalogue, Institut Néerlandais, Paris, October–November, 1980

p. 55 Cesare dell'Acqua, *A Greek Mother*, 1860
Oil on canvas, 100 × 60 cm
Signed and dated
Georges Kouremetis collection, Brussels

The Italian painter Cesare dell'Acqua (1821–1904) never visited Greece, but he did paint a series of pictures depicting contemporary historical events in Greece.

p. 56 Ludwig Vogel, *Portraits of the Greek Refugees in Zürich*, 1823
Pen drawings, 14.8 × 9.2 cm
Schweizerisches Landesmuseum, Zürich

After Ypsilantis's unsuccessful attempt to cross the River Pruth in March 1821, his forces were dispersed. After wandering through Russia, Poland and Germany, 160 of his men – Greeks from Macedonia, Thrace, Epirus and the islands – managed to reach Switzerland in the spring of 1823. There, the Swiss Philhellenic Committee undertook their military training under the supervision of a Major Faezi. It was Faezi who commissioned the Swiss historical painter Ludwig Vogel (1788–1879) to paint their portraits. The plan was to have the portraits lithographed and sold in aid of the Greeks, but it is not known whether this was put into effect. At the same

time, Vogel also began work on a large historical composition, not completed until 1832, when it was exhibited in Zürich. According to contemporary descriptions, it showed a Greek warrior recounting the heroic deeds of the Revolution to a group of boys. One of the models for the painting was the son of Markos Botsaris, whom Vogel had met and drawn in Munich in 1830 (see 'Schweizerische Griechenhilfe 1822–28 im Spiegel der Schweizer Kunst', in *Neue Zürcher Zeitung*, 14 February 1944).

Giovanni Boggi, *Portrait of Theodoros Kolokotronis*, 1825
Sepia drawing, 18 × 14 cm
Museum of the City of Athens

Theodoros Kolokotronis (1770–1843), nicknamed 'The Old Man of the Morea', is a central figure in the history of Greece in the early nineteenth century. He began his long career as 'Fighter of the Turks' by being, alternately, an Armatolos and a Klepht. In 1810 he joined the Greek regiment raised by Sir Richard Church in the Ionian Islands. Throughout the Revolution he was general of the Greek troops in the Morea. During the Bavarian Regency he was imprisoned and sentenced to death, but he was pardoned by King Otho.

Giovanni Boggi (d. 1832) must have visited Greece during the early years of the Revolution, when he drew the portraits of the most eminent of the Greek leaders. He published the following work on Greece: *Collection de portraits des personnages Turcs et Grecs les plus renommés soit par leur cruauté, soit par leur bravoure dans la guerre actuelle de la Grèce, dessinés d'après nature par Boggi*, Paris, 1826–9.

p. 57 Adam Friedel von Friedelsburg, *Portrait of Lascarina Bouboulina*, 1827
From A. de Friedel, *The Greeks: Twenty-four portraits . . . of the principal leaders and personages who have made themselves most conspicuous in the Greek Revolution*, London, 1825–7
Coloured lithograph, 23 × 18.5 cm

Lascarina Bouboulina (1771–1825) was one of the heroines of the War of Independence, Descended from a rich Hydriote family of ship-owners and merchants, she gave her own and her husband's ships to the Greek navy during the Revolution. She took part in many naval battles as captain of her own ship. She was assassinated by a member of her own family

Very little is known about the Danish Philhellene Adam Friedel von Friedelsburg, who called himself Baron Friedel until exposed by a genuine Danish count, Waldamar von Qualen. A friend of Ypsilantis, he was in Greece during the War of Revolution and later settled in London. There he published a series of lithographed portraits *The Greeks: Twenty-four portraits (in four parts of six portraits each) of the principal leaders and personages who have made themselves most conspicuous in the Greek Revolution, with or without biographical descriptions*, 1825–7

BIBLIOGRAPHY: W. St Clair, *That Greece Might Still Be Free*, London, 1972, pp. 89, 376.

p. 58 Bronze clock decorated with a statuette of Konstantinos Kanaris
French, *c.* 1835–40
Angeliki Amandry collection, Athens

Konstantinos Kanaris (1790–1877), a sailor from Psara, became famous as the leader of the attacks with fireships on the Turkish navy. He destroyed the flagship of Captain Pasha in 1822. After the War of Independence he entered politics. He died in office in 1877.

Bronze clock decorated with a scene from the Greek War of Independence
Russian, *c.* 1825–30
Mike Krassakis collection, Cologne

Porcelain vase representing the 'Battle of the Giaour and the Pasha'
Sèvres, 'Empire' style
Georges Kouremetis collection, Brussels

p. 59 Porcelain plate representing the French Philhellenic Committee
French, Mantereau manufacture, *c.* 1830

The title reads 'Greek Committee presided over by M. de Chateaubriand'. Chateaubriand is represented at the top of the table, towards the right.

Music score, 'Le dernier cri des Grecs'
Published in Paris in 1828

The illustration on the title-page appears to be derived from Charles Langlois's painting *The Greeks Receiving the News of the Battle of Navarino* (1827).

The Defeat, after the painting by A. C. H. Vernet
Firescreen, 50 × 40 cm
Georges Kouremetis collection, Brussels

p. 60 George Philip Reinagle, *The Battle of Navarino*, 1827
Oil on canvas, 126 × 203 cm
Exhibited at the Royal Academy, London, in 1829 (424)
Fine Art Society, London

George Philip Reinagle (1802–35) accompanied the English fleet to Greece and painted the Battle of Navarino which, together with other subjects connected with the battle, he exhibited

at the Royal Academy and the British Institution in 1829–31. He also published the following works on Greece: *Illustrations of the Occurrences at the Entrance of the Bay of Patras, between the English Squadron and Turkish Fleets . . . 1827 . . . Dedicated . . . [to] . . . Vice-Admiral Sir Edward Codrington*, London, 1828; *Illustrations of the Battle of Navarin . . . Dedicated . . . [to] . . . H. R. H. the Duke of Clarence*, London, 1828.

George Cruickshank, *The Luncheon of the Great Powers after the Battle of Navarino*, 1827
Coloured lithograph, 24 × 34 cm

The caption to Cruickshank's caricature reads: 'The ALLIED GOURMANDS taking a Luncheon; or the TURKEY in DANGER.' The Russian Admiral Berenski is depicted seated between Sir Edward Codrington and De Rigny; the Austrian representative is watching greedily behind De Rigny's chair. The pictures on the wall are entitled 'Jack in the Seraglio', and 'Bat[tle of] Navorina' (*sic*).

p. 61 Charles Langlois, *The Meeting of General Maison and Ibrahim Pasha by the Bay of Patras*, 1828 (detail)
Lithograph, 23.5 × 19 cm

In August 1828 a French expeditionary force under the command of General Maison was sent to Patras. The French troops took possession of the town on 5 October 1828.

The original painting by Charles Langlois (1789–1870) is now in the Musée de Versailles together with its pendant *The Meeting of General Maison and Ibrahim Pasha at Navarino*. Another Greek painting by Langlois, who never visited Greece, is in the Palais de Compiègne.

p. 62 Anonymous, French, *Coastal Scene in the Morea with Greek and French Soldiers*, 1828
Oil on canvas, 45.5 × 52 cm
Private collection, Munich

'The utter exhaustion of Greece prevented the government of Capodistrias from making any effort to expel the Egyptians from the Peloponnesus. The direct agency of the Allies was required to deliver the country.

'The French government undertook to send an army to expel Ibrahim, for the mutual jealousies of England and Russia threatened otherwise to retard the pacification of Greece indefinitely. On the 19th July 1828 a protocol was signed, accepting the offer of France; and on the 30th August an army of fourteen thousand men, under the command of General Maison, landed at Petalidi in the Gulf of Coron. The convention concluded by Codrington at

Alexandria had been ineffectual. It required the imposing force of the French general to compel Ibrahim to sign a new convention for the immediate evacuation of the Morea. This convention was signed on the 7th of September 1828, and the first division of the Egyptian army, consisting of five thousand five hundred men, sailed from Navarin on the 16th . . . Navarin, Modon and Coron fell into the hands of the French . . . France thus gained the honour of delivering Greece from the last of her conquerors, and she increased the debt of gratitude by the admirable conduct of the French soldiers' (George Finlay, *A History of Greece from its Conquest by the Romans to the Present Time*, London, 1857, vol. VII, pp. 26–7).

p. 64 Karl Friedrich von Schinkel, *Project for a Royal Palace on the Acropolis*, 1834
From K. F. von Schinkel, *Entwurf zu einem Königspalast auf der Akropolis zu Athen*, Berlin, 1878
Coloured lithograph, 32 × 75 cm

Karl Friedrich von Schinkel (1781–1841) never visited Greece. A friend of Maximilian, Crown Prince of Bavaria, he was asked by him to make a plan for a Royal Palace on the Acropolis at Athens for Maximilian's brother Otho. The plan was never carried out.

Schinkel published the following works on Greece: *Entwurf zu einem Königspalast auf der Akropolis zu Athen. Für die Ausführung erfunden von Karl Friedrich Schinkel. Vierte Ausgabe*, Berlin, 1878; *Sammlung architektonischer Entwürfe, enthaltend theils Werke, welche ausgeführt sind, theils Gegenstände, deren Ausführung beabsichtigt wurde*, Berlin, 1828–40.

BIBLIOGRAPHY: 'Schinkels Traum von einen Königspalast auf der Akropolis zu Athen', in *Atlantis*, 6 (1934), pp. 129–34; Paul Ortwin Rave, *Ein Blick in Griechenlands Blüte*, Berlin, 1946; R. Carter, 'K. F. Schinkel's Project for a Royal Palace on the Acropolis', in *Journal of the Society of Architectural Historians* (USA) XXXVIII, 1 (March 1979), pp. 34–46.

p. 65 Peter von Hess, *King Otho's Arrival in Nafplion on 6 February 1833*, 1839
Oil on canvas, 273 × 416 cm
Bayerische Staatsgemäldesammlungen, Munich

'King Otho quitted the English frigate which conveyed him to Greece on the 6th February 1833. His entry into Nauplia was a spectacle well calculated to inspire the Greeks with enthusiasm . . .

'The scene itself formed a splendid picture . . . Greeks and Albanians, mountaineers and islanders, soldiers, sailors, and peasants, in their varied and picturesque dresses, hailed the young monarch ... Families in bright attire glided in boats over the calm sea amidst the gaily decorated frigates of the Allied squadrons. The music of many bands in the ships and on the shore enlivened the scene, and the roar of artillery in every direction gave an imposing pomp to the ceremony. The uniforms of many armies and navies, and the sounds of many languages, testified that most civilized nations had sent deputies to inaugurate the festival of the regeneration of Greece.

'Nature was in perfect harmony. The sun was warm, and the air balmy with the breath of spring, while a light breeze wafted freshness from the sea. The landscape was beautiful, and it recalled memories of a glorious past. The white buildings of the Turkish town of Nauplia clustered at the foot of the Venetian fortifications and cyclopean foundations that crown its rocky promontory. The mountain citadel of Palamedes frowned over both, and the island fort of Burdjé, memorable in the history of the Revolution, stood like a sentinel in the harbour' (George Finlay, *A History of Greece from its Conquest by the Romans to the Present Time*, London, 1857, vol. VII, pp. 104–5).

Peter von Hess (1792–1871) accompanied King Otho to Greece in January 1833 and spent the next nine months there, working on a commission from Ludwig I of Bavaria to record Otho's arrival and also to make a series of historical paintings of events during the War of Revolution. Works by Hess are to be found in the Neue Pinakothek, Stadtmuseum and Graphische Sammlung, Munich. His series from the War of Revolution was published in a series of lithographic prints as *Die Befreiung Griechenlands in 39 Bildern, entworfen von Peter Hess*.
BIBLIOGRAPHY: B. Reinhardt, *Der Münchner Schlachten- und Genremaler Peter von Hess*, Munich, 1977; M. Papanikolaou, 'Portraits of the Warriors of 1821 by Peter von Hess' (in Greek), in *Zygos*, 39 (January–February 1980), pp. 86–90).

Peter von Hess, *King Otho Received by the Greek Patriarch at the Theseum on 13 January 1835*, 1835
Oil on canvas, 250 × 410 cm
Bayerische Staatsgemäldesammlungen, Munich

p. 66 Alexandre Marie Colin, *Landscape with a Greek Boy*, 1831
Oil on canvas, 44 × 36 cm
Benaki Museum, Athens

The French painter Alexandre Marie Colin (1798–1873) never visited Greece. In the 1820s he was a member of the

circle of Romantic painters working in Paris that included Delacroix, Géricault and Bonington, all three of whom feature in portraits sketched by him. He was particularly intimate with Bonington, but all Bonington's letters to him were later destroyed by his son. In 1825 the two friends spent some months in London, and shared lodgings at no. 7 Acton Street off the Gray's Inn Road. Colin exhibited various subjects after Byron's poems at the Galerie Lebrun in 1826. An accomplished lithographer, he made many lithographs after Géricault's works. See also *Historical Illustrations of Lord Byron's Works in a Series of Etchings, by Reveil, from Original Paintings, by A. Colin*, London, Charles Tilt, 1833.

A Young Greek Defending his Wounded Father, after the painting by Ary Scheffer
Tapestry panel, 320 × 200 cm
Private collection, Athens

See also illustration on p. 54 above.

p. 67 Charles Lock Eastlake, *Greek Fugitives*, 1833
Oil on canvas, 95 × 134 cm
Exhibited at the Royal Academy, London, in 1833
Benaki Museum, Athens

William Finden describes this work in his *Royal Gallery of British Art* (1838): 'The picture may be considered to represent an episode of that devastating war, in which, driven from their hearths, the unfortunate Greeks sometimes found safety on board the British ships stationed on the coast, and which were on the watch to succour them ... Mr Eastlake has painted his conception of such a scene of danger and suffering, and excited in the breast of every observer a deep interest in the fate of the personage of his drama.'

Lodovico Lipparini, *An Old Greek Warrior*, 1842
Pencil drawing, 9 × 13 cm
Signed and dated
Benaki Museum, Athens

p. 68 Anonymous, French, *French Tourists Visiting the Acropolis*, c. 1860
Gouache, 25 × 40 cm
Georges Kouremetis collection, Brussels

The middle rider is the Director of the *Figaro*.

p. 69 John Linton, *Shepherd and Shepherdess*, c. 1850
Oil on canvas, 22 × 30 cm
Benaki Museum, Athens

The Acropolis is shown in the distance surrounded by imaginary classical buildings. The relief in the left fore-

ground is decorated with a pastoral theme.

p. 70 Ludwig Köllnberger, *The Famous Athenian Coffee-house 'Orea Hellas'*, 1837
Watercolour, 20 × 20 cm
National Historical Museum, Athens

The scene is a microcosm of Athenian society during the Othonian period. The group of men on the right wearing the 'fustanella' are *pallikars* (ex-warriors); on the left are Westernized Greeks, wearing Frankish costume; and at the far left are some Bavarian soldiers. The billiard-table in the centre must have been one of the first in Athens. Coffee-houses have played an important role in the political life of modern Greece. The 'Orea Hellas' (Beautiful Greece) coffee-house, for instance, where foreign newspapers were available, was the source of many of the political uprisings in Greece during the Othonian period.
Ludwig Köllnberger (1811–1892) was sent to Greece in 1833 as a subaltern in the Bavarian army and served there until 1838. There is a set of watercolours by him in the National Historical Museum, Athens.
BIBLIOGRAPHY: I. Meletopoulos, *The Early Years of the Othonian Period as Illustrated in the Watercolours by Köllnberger* (in Greek), Athens, 1976

p. 73 Ludwig Thiersch, *Portrait of a Greek Lady*, c. 1870
Oil on canvas, 124 × 83 cm
National Gallery, Athens

The sitter is Kleoniki, sister of Ioannes Gennadios, the Greek scholar and diplomat (1844–1932).
Ludwig Thiersch (1825–1909), the son of the Philhellene F. Thiersch, went to Athens in 1852. He spent three years there as Professor of Painting in the School of Fine Arts. Some of his works are now in the National Gallery, Athens. Thiersch painted the fresco decorations in the Russian Church, Athens (1854–5); the Greek Church of the Holy Trinity, Vienna (1856); the Greek Church of Haghia Sophia, Manchester (1880–1); and the Greek Church of St Stephen, Paris (1892).
BIBLIOGRAPHY: D. Papastamos, *The Effect of Nazarene Thought on Modern Greek Church Painting* (in Greek), Athens, 1977.

p. 74 Gustave Doré, *Scene with Greek Bandits*
From Edmond About, *Le Roi des montagnes*, 5th edition, Paris, 1861
Etching

p. 75 Gustave Doré, *Scene with Greek Bandits*
From Edmond About, *Le Roi des montagnes*, 5th edition, Paris, 1861
Etching

p.76 Jean Léon Gérome, *The Atelier of Tanagra, c.* 1850
Oil on canvas, 74 × 104 cm
Fine Art Society, London

Jean Leon Gérome (1824–1904) was one of the leaders of the Neo-Greek School in France.

p. 77 Lord Leighton, *Greek Girls Playing at Ball*, 1889
Oil on canvas, 74 × 78 cm
Dick Institute, Kilmarnock

Frederick, Lord Leighton (1830–96) visited Rhodes and Athens in 1867. After his return to England he painted many works with classical subjects.
BIBLIOGRAPHY: Leonée and Richard Ormond, *Lord Leighton*, London, 1975.

PART II

Plates 1–6 (pp. 82–87)

1 Joseph Cartwright, *The Town and Citadel of Corfu*, 1820
Watercolour, 21 × 35.5 cm
Benaki Museum, Athens

Joseph Cartwright (1789–1829) was Paymaster-General to the British garrison at Corfu in 1816–20. He published his *Views in the Ionian Islands* in 1821, and *Selections of the Costume of Albania and Greece* in 1822. The largest series of his watercolour views of Greece and the Ionian Islands is in the Benaki Museum, Athens.
BIBLIOGRAPHY: Joseph Cartwright, *Views in the Ionian Islands*, with an introductory note by A. Delivorrias and F. M. Tsigakou, Athens, 1980.

2 John Frederick Lewis, *Distant View of the Citadel of Corfu*, 1840
Watercolour, 25 × 40.5 cm
Inscribed 'Corfu J. F. Lewis July 14 1840'
British Museum, London

John Frederick Lewis (1805–76) visited Corfu and Epirus in 1840 while on his way to Asia Minor.
BIBLIOGRAPHY: Hugh Stokes, 'J. F. Lewis', in *Walker's Quarterly*, 1929.

3 Edward Lear, *Capo Ducato, or Sappho's Leap in Santa Maura (Leucas)*, 1863
From E. Lear, *Views in the Seven Ionian Islands*, London, 1863, pl. XI
Lithotint, 23.5 × 36.5 cm

Edward Lear (1812–88) first visited Greece in 1848–9. In 1855–8 and again in 1861–4 he was resident in Corfu. Lear travelled extensively in Greece, and by the time he returned to England in 1864 he had made over 2,000 drawings of views and subjects in Greece. Lear's work constitutes the most complete record we possess of the Greek landscape in the mid-nineteenth century.

The majority of his works are now at Harvard, and in the Benaki Museum and Gennadeios Library, Athens, and the Museum of the City of Athens. Works by Lear may also be found in many private collections in England and Greece.

There are two publications on Greece by Lear: *Journals of a Landscape Painter in Albania, &c*, London, 1851, and *Views in the Seven Ionian Islands*, London, 1863.
BIBLIOGRAPHY: Lady Strachey (ed.), *Letters of Edward Lear*, London, 1907, and *Later Letters of Edward Lear*, London, 1911; Vivien Noakes, *Edward Lear. The Life of a Wanderer*, London, 1968; F. M. Tsigakou, 'Edward Lear in Greece', unpublished M. Phil. thesis, University College, London, 1977.

4 Edward Dodwell, *View of Ithaca*, 1801
From E. Dodwell, *Views in Greece*, London, 1821
Coloured aquatint, 25 × 40 cm

Edward Dodwell (1767–1832) visited Greece in 1801 and again in 1804–6. He published the following works on Greece: *A Classical and Topographical Tour through Greece*, 2 vols, London, 1819; *Views in Greece*, London, 1821.

5 Edward Lear, *View of Parga*, 1864
Oil on panel, 17.8 × 28 cm
Signed in monogram and dated
Private collection, London

6 Edward Lear, *The Rocks of Suli*, 1849
Watercolour and gouache, 16 × 25 cm
Inscribed 'Suli 1849' and signed in monogram
Ashmolean Museum, Oxford

Colour Plates VIII–XIV (pp. 88–97)

VIII Joseph Schranz, *The Town and Citadel of Corfu from the Port, c.* 1840
Oil on canvas, 33 × 49 cm
Museum of the City of Athens

Little is known about Joseph Schranz, apart from the fact that he was Maltese and came from a family of artists. Schranz visited Crete in 1834 with Robert Pashley, and he must also have visited the Ionian Islands and Athens at some time since there are many paintings by him of views in those places in the Benaki Museum, Athens, the Museum of the City of Athens, and in private collections in Greece. Views by Schranz appear as illustrations in: Robert Pashley, *Travels in Crete*, 2 vols, London, 1837; Captain T. A. B. Spratt, *Travels and Researches in Crete*, 2 vols, London, 1865.

IX Edward Lear, *View of the Town of Zante from the Castle Hill*, 1863
Pencil, pen and watercolour, 35.8 × 53.9 cm
Inscribed 'not possible to draw for flies. I being obliged to sit in the sunshine. Zante. 26 May. 1863.'
Fine Art Society, London

X Edward Lear, *View of Argostoli in Cephalonia*, 1864
Oil on canvas, 68.6 × 113 cm
Signed in monogram and dated
Fine Art Society, London

XI William Gell, *The Valley of Tempe*, 1805
Watercolour, 18.5 × 26.5 cm
Benaki Museum, Athens

XII Edward Lear, *The Monastery of Dionysiou, Mount Athos*, 1862
Oil on canvas, 67 × 112 cm
Signed in monogram and dated
Museum of the City of Athens

XIII Edward Lear, *View of Mount Parnassus and the Plains of Boeotia*, 1862
Oil on panel, 24.5 × 38.5 cm
Signed in monogram and dated
Private collection

XIV Karl Rottmann, *The Plain of Chaeronea and Lake Copais*, 1835
Watercolour, 25.9 × 36.2 cm
Staatliche Graphische Sammlung, Munich

Karl Rottmann (1797–1850) was in Greece in 1834–5, commissioned to execute a series of landscapes to decorate the gallery of the Royal Gardens in Munich.

Plates 7–34 (pp. 98–127)

7 William Haygarth, *View of Ioannina*, 1810
Sepia and watercolour, 17.5 × 25 cm
Dated 'Aug. 1810'
Gennadeios Library, Athens

Very little is known about William Haygarth (1784–1825). He visited Greece in 1810–11, and in 1814 he published *Greece, a Poem, in Three Parts; with Notes, Classical Illustrations, and Sketches of the Scenery*. The original sepia drawings for Haygarth's book are now in the Gennadeios Library, Athens, together with a sketchbook of 1811.
BIBLIOGRAPHY: T. Spencer, *Fair Greece, Sad Relic*, Bath, 1974, p. 281; M. C. Magnin, 'De la Grèce véritable', in *Causeries et méditations historiques et littéraires*, vol. II, 1843, pp. 1–10.

8 William Page, *The Lake of Ioannina, c.* 1820
From *Finden's Illustrations to Murray's*

First Complete and Uniform Edition of the Life and Works of Lord Byron, 17 vols, London, 1832–4
Engraving, 8.5 × 13.5 cm

It is not known exactly when William Page (1794–1879) visited Greece, but it must have been before 1822.
BIBLIOGRAPHY: J. H. Money, 'The Life and Work of William Page', *Old Watercolour Society Club*, 1972 (includes a catalogue of Page's Greek works); C. W. J. Eliot, 'Lord Byron, Father Paul and the Artist William Page', in *Hesperia: Journal of the American School of Classical Studies at Athens*, XLIV, 4 (October–December 1975), pp. 409–25.

9 Charles Robert Cockerell, *A Greek House in Ioannina*, 1811
From The Rev. Thomas Smart Hughes, *Travels in Sicily, Greece and Albania*, London, 1820, vol. I
Etching, 18 × 23.5 cm

10 Edward Lear, *View of Meteora*, 1848/63
Watercolour heightened with white, 16.5 × 25.4 cm
Signed in monogram and dated '1848 1863'
Private collection

11 Otto Magnus von Stackelberg, *The Monastery of Varlaam at Meteora*, 1812
From O. M. von Stackelberg, *La Grèce. Vues pittoresques et topographiques*, Paris, 1834
Lithograph, 32 × 25 cm

Otto Magnus, Baron von Stackelberg (1787–1837), travelled to Greece in 1810 in the company of Haller von Hallerstein. In the spring of 1811 he made a brief tour of Asia Minor and returned to Greece in 1812, where he remained until 1814. He published the following works on Greece: *Der Apollotempel zu Bassae in Arkadien und die daselbst ausgegraben Bildwerke*, Rome, 1826; *Costumes et usages des peuples de la Grèce moderne*, Rome, 1825; *Trachten und Gebräuche der Neugriechen*, Berlin, 1831; *La Grèce. Vues pittoresques et topographiques*, Paris, 1834; *Die Gräber der Hellenen*, Berlin, 1837.
BIBLIOGRAPHY: G. Rodenwaldt, *O. M. von Stackelberg, der Entdecker der griechischen Landschaft*, Munich/Berlin, 1957.

12 Joseph Cartwright, *View of Larissa and the River Peneus*, 1820
Watercolour, 42 × 64 cm
Benaki Museum, Athens

13 Simone Pomardi, *The Village of Portaria on Mount Pelion*, 1806
From Edward Dodwell, *Views in Greece*, London, 1821
Coloured aquatint, 25 × 31 cm

Simone Pomardi (1760–1830), a water-colour painter, went to Greece at the turn of the nineteenth century, and was one of the many draughtsmen who made a living by furnishing travellers with records of the scenery and classical monuments.
BIBLIOGRAPHY: E. Dodwell, *A Classical and Topographical Tour through Greece*, London, 1819, vol. II, p. 457.

14 Edward Lear, *View of Salonica (Thessaloniki) and the Thermaic Gulf*, 1848
Watercolour and gouache, 17.5 × 37.5 cm
Signed in monogram
Ashmolean Museum, Oxford

15 Edward Lear, *The Monastery of Koutloumoussiou, Mount Athos*, 1856
Watercolour heightened with white, 33.7 × 50.8 cm
Inscribed 'Koutloumousi. Sept. 1. 1856. (2)'
Private collection, Oxford

16 Hugh William Williams, *A Street in Patras*, 1817
Watercolour, 35.8 × 49.8 cm
Benaki Museum, Athens

Hugh William Williams (1773–1829) made an extensive tour of Greece in 1817 and published the following works on the country: *Travels in Italy, Greece and the Ionian Islands, in a Series of Letters*, 2 vols, Edinburgh, 1820; *Select Views in Greece*, Edinburgh, 1827–8. In 1822 he held an exhibition of his Greek pictures in Edinburgh (see *Views in Greece, Italy, Sicily, and the Ionian Islands, Painted in Watercolours by H. W. Williams*, exhibition catalogue, Calton Convening Rooms, Waterloo Place, Edinburgh, 1822). The majority of Williams's Greek pictures are now in the National Gallery of Scotland, Edinburgh.
BIBLIOGRAPHY: William Hazlitt, *Essays on the Fine Arts*, ed. W. C. Hazlitt, London, 1873, pp. 141–4; D. and F. Irwin, *Scottish Painters*, London, 1975.

17 William Purser, *View of Missolonghi with Lord Byron's House*, 1824
Watercolour, 14 × 22 cm
Signed on the back and dated '21 May 1824'
Benaki Museum, Athens

The British architect William Purser (c. 1790–1834) travelled in Italy and Greece from 1817 to 1820.
BIBLIOGRAPHY: H. M. Colvin, *A Biographical Dictionary of English Architects, 1660–1840*, London, 1954.

18 Edward Dodwell, *Dinner in a Greek House at Crissa*, 1801
Watercolour, 26 × 40 cm
Benaki Museum, Athens

An engraving of this scene appears in Dodwell's *Views in Greece*, London, 1821, pl. 2.

19 Edward Lear, *View of the Village of Kastri, Delphi*, 1849
Pen and watercolour, 40.6 × 50.6 cm
Inscribed 'Delphi. April 16. 1849.'
Gennadeios Library, Athens

20 André Louis de Sinety, *The Castalian Spring at Delphi*, 1847
From *Voyage de S. A. R. Monseigneur le duc de Montpensier à Tunis, en Egypte, en Turquie et en Grèce*, Paris, 1847
Coloured lithograph, 43.5 × 26.5 cm

The French naval officer André Louis de Sinety visited Greece in 1845–6 as the captain of the ship *Gomer* in which the Duc de Montpensier, the son of King Louis-Philippe, was making a Mediterranean cruise. The sketches De Sinety made on this tour appeared as a series of lithographs under the title *Voyage de S. A. R. Monseigneur le duc de Montpensier à Tunis, en Egypte, en Turquie et en Grèce*, by Antoine de Latour, Paris, 1847. Most of his original sketches are now in a private collection in Athens.

21 John Fulleylove, *Stoa of the Athenians at Delphi*, 1895
Pencil and watercolour, 19.3 × 27.9 cm
Signed and dated '6 May /95'
Fine Art Society, London

John Fulleylove (1847–1908) visited Greece in 1895. He exhibited a Greek subject at the Royal Academy in 1898.
BIBLIOGRAPHY: *Catalogue of the Work by the Late J. Fulleylove, R.I.*, Langham Chambers, London, 1908 (sale catalogue).

22 William Walker, *View of Levadia*, 1803
From W. Walker, *Six Picturesque Views of Greece*, London, 1804
Coloured aquatint, 38 × 50 cm

William Walker (1780–1868) visited Greece in 1803 with the architect Robert Smirke. He exhibited eighteen Greek subjects at the Royal Academy: in 1805, 1807, 1829, 1830 and 1833.
BIBLIOGRAPHY: J. L. Roget, *A History of the 'Old Watercolour' Society*, London, 1891, vol. I, pp. 357–8.

23 Hugh William Williams, *View of Thebes*, 1819
Watercolour, 48 × 70 cm
Signed and dated
Benaki Museum, Athens (presented by Sir Steven Runciman)

24 Théodore du Moncel, *View of Eleusis*, c. 1843
From Th. du Moncel, *De Venise à Constantinople à travers la Grèce*, Paris, [1843?], pl. 25

Coloured lithograph, 25 × 38 cm

Théodore Achille Louis Vicomte du Moncel (1821–84) visited Greece in 1843 and again in 1845. He exhibited Greek subjects at the Salon in 1846–9, and published the following illustrated works' on Greece: *Excursion par terre d'Athènes a Nauplie*, Paris, [1845?]; *Vues pittoresques des monuments d'Athènes*, Paris, 1845; *De Venise à Constantinople à travers la Grèce*, Paris, [1843?].

25 Raffaello Ceccoli, *View of the Acropolis with the Theatre of Herodes Atticus*, c. 1850
Oil on canvas, 60.5 × 80.5 cm
National Gallery, Athens

Very little is known of the Italian artist Raffaello Ceccoli, who went to Corfu in 1839 because of his daughter's ill-health. They remained in the Ionian Islands until 1843, when Ceccoli moved his daughter to the island of Poros, while he himself took up the post of teacher of painting at the School of Fine Arts, Athens. Ceccoli's daughter died in 1849, and he returned to Italy in 1852.

There is a portrait by him of his daughter in the Monastery of Poros, and some views of Athens and portraits of the heroes of the Revolution in the National Gallery and the Benaki Museum, Athens.

26 Henry Cook, *View of Athens from the Road to Eleusis*, 1850
Watercolour, 42 × 68 cm
Private collection, Athens

The English architect Henry Cook made a brief visit to Greece in 1850 while on his way to Constantinople. He published a series of articles on 'The Present State of the Monuments of Greece' in the *Art Journal*, 1851, pp. 130–2, 187–8, 228–9, and a folio volume entitled *Recollections of a Tour in the Ionian Islands, Greece and Constantinople*, 1853.

27 William Page, *View of the Acropolis*, c. 1820
Watercolour, 28 × 40 cm
Signed on the verso
Private collection, Athens

28 Hugh William Williams, *The Parthenon*, 1819
Watercolour, 80 × 115 cm
Signed
Private collection, Athens

29 Hugh William Williams, *View of the Erechtheum*, 1819
Watercolour, 80 × 115 cm
Signed
Private collection, Athens

30 Ippolito Caffi, *The Propylaea*, 1843
Oil on canvas, 23 × 31 cm

Signed and dated
Museo d'Arte Moderna Ca' Pesaro, Venice

Ippolito Caffi (1809–66) visited Athens briefly in 1838 on his way to the Middle East and Egypt, and again in 1843 on his way back to Italy. A set of his views of Athens is in the Museo d'Arte Moderna Ca' Pesaro, Venice.
BIBLIOGRAPHY: Commune di Venezia, Assessorato alla Cultura ed alle Belle Arti (ed.), *Ippolito Caffi (1809–66)*, with an introduction by Guido Perocco, Venice, 1979.

31 Ippolito Caffi, *Interior of the Parthenon*, 1843 (detail)
Oil on canvas, 23 × 34 cm
Signed and dated
Museo d'Arte Moderna Ca' Pesaro, Venice

32 Ippolito Caffi, *The Parthenon and the Erechtheum*, 1843
Oil on canvas, 36.5 × 60.5 cm
Signed and dated
Museo d'Arte Moderna Ca' Pesaro, Venice

33 J. N. H. de Chacaton, *The Temple of Apteros Nike (Wingless Victory)*, 1839
Watercolour, 22 × 37 cm
Benaki Museum, Athens

Jean Nicolas Henri de Chacaton (b. 1813) was in Athens in c. 1838–9. He exhibited one Greek work at the Salon of 1846. There is a set of watercolours by him in the Benaki Museum, Athens.
BIBLIOGRAPHY: The Hon. Mrs G. L. Dawson Damer, *Diary of a Tour in Greece, Turkey, Egypt and the Holy Land*, London, 1841, introduction.

34 Carl Haag, *View of the Acropolis*, 1861 (detail)
Watercolour, 98.4 × 60.3 cm
Signed and dated
Private collection, London

It is not clear whether Carl Haag (1820–1915) visited Greece, but if he did it was either during his visit to Dalmatia and Montenegro in 1854, or that to Egypt and Asia Minor in 1858–60.
BIBLIOGRAPHY: *The Rediscovery of Greece*, exhibition catalogue, Fine Art Society, London, 1979.

Colour Plates XV–XXII (pp. 128–137)

XV Johann Jacob Wolfensberger, *View of Athens from the Ilissus*, 1834
Oil on panel, 22.5 × 29.5 cm
Private collection, Athens

Johann Jacob Wolfensberger (1797–1850) visited Athens in 1832, stayed for two years, and then made a tour of Asia Minor in 1834. On his return to Zürich he exhibited some 200 watercolours of

Greece and Asia Minor. Greek works by Wolfensberger may be found in the Musée des Beaux Arts, Zürich.

Wolfensberger contributed illustrations to the following publications: G. N. Wright, *The Shores and Islands of the Mediterranean*, 2 vols, London, 1840, and *The Rhine, Italy and Greece*, 2 vols, London, 1840; J. Sherer, *The Classic Lands of Europe . . . with the Southern Shore of the Mediterranean*, 2 vols, London, 1879–81.

XVI Hugh William Williams, *View of the Propylaea*, 1819
Watercolour, 85 × 120 cm
Signed and dated
Private collection, Athens

XVII Jean Baptiste Hilaire, *A Marriage in Athens*, c. 1800
Gouache, 57.5 × 64.5 cm
Signed lower left
Stavros Niarchos collection

Jean Baptiste Hilaire (1753–1822) was in Greece during 1776–7 as a member of Choiseul-Gouffier's expedition to the Aegean Islands. He was responsible for most of the illustrations in Choiseul-Gouffier's *Voyage pittoresque de la Grèce*, 3 vols, Paris, 1782–1822. Works by Hilaire with Greek subjects may be found in the Benaki Museum and the National Historical Museum, Athens.

XVIII Théodore Aligny, *Greek Girls Dancing the 'Romaika'*, 1850
Oil on canvas, 111 × 75 cm
Museum of the City of Athens

Claude François Théodore Aligny (1798–1871) was sent by the French government to Greece in 1844 to execute a series of drawings of the classical sites. In 1845 he published *Vues des sites les plus célèbres de la Grèce antique dessinées sur nature . . .*
BIBLIOGRAPHY: Facsimile edition of the *Vues*, with an introduction by P. Prevelakis (in Greek), Athens, 1971.

XIX Charles Lock Eastlake, *The Erechtheum*, 1820
Oil on canvas, 64.7 × 87.6 cm
Commissioned by Frederick North, fifth Earl of Guildford
Sir Ellis Waterhouse collection

XX J. N. H. de Chacaton, *Hadrian's Library*, 1839
Watercolour, 22.5 × 35.5 cm
Benaki Museum, Athens

XXI Vicenzo Lanza, *View of the Area around the Theseum*, 1869
Watercolour, 24 × 35 cm
Benaki Museum, Athens

Vicenzo Lanza (1822–1902), a teacher in the Academy of Fine Arts at Venice, fled to Greece in 1848 as a political refugee. When established in Athens, he was much patronized by King Otho and Queen Amalia. From 1863 to 1900 he was a Professor in the School of Fine Arts, and also held the post of Professor of Painting in the Military Academy, Athens.

Lanza was a very popular artist in Greece in the second half of the nineteenth century. There are Greek works by him in the National Gallery and the Benaki Museum, Athens, and in many private collections in Greece. He also worked on the frescoes in the Russian Church in Athens. There are illustrations by Lanza in W. M. Wyse (ed.), *An Excursion in the Peloponnesus in the Year 1858*, 2 vols, London, 1865.
BIBLIOGRAPHY: S. Lydakis, *A Dictionary of Greek Painters and Printers* (in Greek), Athens, 1976, p. 441.

XXII James Skene, *View of Kephissia*, 1839
Watercolour, 26 × 52 cm
Inscribed 'Kephissia & Pentelicus, Oct. 1839'
National Historical Museum, Athens

James Skene (1775–1864) lived in Athens in 1828–45. His son Henry married Princess Rhalou Rizos-Rangavis of a Phanariot family of Athens; his daughter Caroline married Alexandros, Rhalou's brother, a statesman and man of letters.

A large number of watercolours by Skene in family possession were donated to the National Historical Museum, Athens, in 1967. At the same time, his journals in Greece were donated to the Greek Academy. There is also a set of Greek drawings by Skene in the British Museum, London.
BIBLIOGRAPHY: *Views of Greece by James Skene*, catalogue of an exhibition arranged by the Anglo-Hellenic League to mark its jubilee, 1913–1963, London, 1963.

Plates 35–69 (pp. 138–167)

35 Ferdinand Stademann, *A Panoramic View of Athens*, 1835
From F. Stademann, *Panorama von Athen*, Munich, 1841
Lithograph, 45 × 95 cm

Ferdinand Stademann (1791–1872) went to Greece in 1832 and was commissioned by King Otho to execute a series of panoramic views of Athens which he published in Munich in 1841 under the title *Panorama von Athen*. There are Greek works by Stademann in the Stadtmuseum, Munich.

36 Karl Wilhelm von Heydeck, *View of the Parthenon with the Church of the Virgin*, 1834
Watercolour, 45 × 60 cm
Signed in monogram and dated
Benaki Museum, Athens

Karl Wilhelm Freiherr von Heideck (Heydeck) or Heidegger (1788–1861) first went to Greece in 1826 as Commander of the corps of military advisers sent by Ludwig to instruct the Greeks in the tactics of the war. He returned to Greece in 1833 as one of the three Bavarian Regents who accompanied Otho. His works on Greek subjects are in the Neue Pinakothek, Munich, and in the Museum of the City of Athens. Heydeck published the following work on Greece: 'Die bayerische Philhellenenfahrt 1826–29', in *Darstellungen aus der bayerischen Kriegs- und Heeresgeschichte*, vol. 6 (1897), p. 1 *et seq.*
BIBLIOGRAPHY: J. M. Forster, 'Die bayerische Expedition nach Griechenland', in *Das Bayerland*, vol. 2 (1891), p. 244.

37 Thomas Hartley Cromek, *The Olympieum*, 1844
Watercolour, 43 × 67 cm
Signed and dated
Museum of the City of Athens

Thomas Hartley Cromek (1809–73) visited Greece in 1834 and again in 1845.
BIBLIOGRAPHY: *Thomas Hartley Cromek, 1809–1873. Exhibition of watercolours and drawings of Italy, Greece and the Mediterranean*, exhibition catalogue, P. and D. Colnaghi, London, 1972.

38 Alfred Beaumont, *The Choragic Monument of Lysicrates*, 1834
Pen and watercolour, 21.5 × 48.5 cm
Inscribed 'Coragic Monument of Lysicrates'
Museum of the City of Athens

Little is known about the English architect Alfred Beaumont (active in the 1830s). He was in Athens in 1834 and subsequently exhibited views of Greek buildings at the Royal Academy, London in 1838. A set of drawings by Beaumont was exhibited at the Fine Art Society, London, in 1979 (see exhibition catalogue, *The Rediscovery of Greece*).

39 Ippolito Caffi, *Hadrian's Gate*, 1844 (detail)
Oil on canvas, 22 × 36 cm
Signed and dated
Museo d'Arte Moderna Ca' Pesaro, Venice

40 Ippolito Caffi, *The Theatre of Herodes Atticus*, 1843
Oil on canvas, 26 × 58 cm
Signed and dated
Museo d'Arte Moderna Ca' Pesaro, Venice

41 Thomas Hartley Cromek, *The Hill of the Areopagus*, 1846
Watercolour, 23 × 48 cm
Inscribed 'Areopagus. Novr. 1846.'
Private collection

42 Ippolito Caffi, *The Agora Gate*, 1843

Oil on canvas, 24 × 33 cm
Signed and dated
Museo d'Arte Moderna Ca' Pesaro, Venice

43 Sebastiano Ittar, *Fête with a Tightrope Walker by the Theseum*, 1800
Sepia wash and ink, 15 × 23 cm
Signed, dated, and inscribed 'Ballo incorda rapresentato in Atene nella piazza di Teseo'
Private collection, London

Sebastiano Ittar (active c. 1800) was one of the group of artists recruited in Italy by William R. Hamilton, Lord Elgin's private secretary, to work on the Acropolis of Athens. The party remained in Athens for three years, 1800–3. There is a set of Greek drawings by Ittar in the British Museum, London.
BIBLIOGRAPHY: A. H. Smith, 'Lord Elgin and his Collection', in *Journal of Hellenic Studies*, XXXVI (1916), pp. 173–5; W. St Clair, *Lord Elgin and the Marbles*, London, 1967, pp. 30–1.

44 Joseph Scherer, *Greek Dance in Athens*, 1849
Pencil drawing, 27.5 × 22.5 cm
Benaki Museum, Athens

Joseph Scherer (1814–91) made a tour of Greece and Asia Minor in 1842–4. In 1842 he was working on the fresco decorations in the Royal Palace in Athens. There is an extensive collection of Scherer's views and street scenes in the Benaki Museum, Athens.

45 J. P. E. F. Peytier, *An Athenian Quarter*, 1833
Watercolour, 35.6 × 51.6 cm
Private collection, Athens

Jean Pierre Eugène Félicien Peytier (1793–1864), a military engineer, was sent to Greece by the French government in 1828 in order to train Greek engineers. The following year he joined the French Scientific Expedition to the Morea as a cartographer. During 1833–6 he was working on a map of the Greek Kingdom, commissioned by the Greek government, which was published in 1852.
BIBLIOGRAPHY: S. Papadopoulos and A. Karakatsani, *Liberated Greece and the Scientific Expedition of the Morea: The Peytier Folio* (in Greek), Athens, 1971.

46 Ernst Ziller, *Designs for Two Athenian Villas*, 1895
Watercolour, 39 × 56 cm
National Gallery, Athens

Ernst Ziller (1837–1923) went to Greece in 1861, where he supervised the construction of the Athens Academy. He returned to Athens in 1868. The most fashionable architect of his day, he designed a series of public buildings and private houses throughout Greece.

The largest collection of his Greek designs is now in the National Gallery, Athens.
BIBLIOGRAPHY: D. Papastamos, *Ernst Ziller* (in Greek), Athens, 1973.

47 Leo von Klenze, *Project for the Church of St Dionysius Areopagites*, 1844
Watercolour, 47.5 × 70.5 cm
Museum of the City of Athens

Leo von Klenze (1784–1864) was sent to Greece by Ludwig I of Bavaria in 1834 and spent three months in Athens. During his stay he simplified the grandiose plan of Athens that had been drawn up by the architects S. Kleanthis and E. Schaubert, suggested alterations to the plan of Piraeus, and undertook the plan for the Royal Palace and the Church of St Dionysius Areopagites. He made a thorough study for the protection of the antiquities in Athens, his main interest being the Acropolis. Klenze was also one of the first to remark on and to study the asymmetry occurring in the ancient buildings of the Acropolis, such as the Propylaea and the Erechtheum. He published the following work on Greece: *Aphoristische Bemerkungen gesammelt auf seiner Reise nach Griechenland*, Berlin, 1838.
BIBLIOGRAPHY: F. von Quast, *Mitteilungen über Alt- and Neuathen*, Berlin, 1834; *Leipziger Illustrirte Zeitung*, 26 (1856), no. 675, pp. 380–1; A. Miliarakes, 'A Ceremony on the Acropolis of Athens' (in Greek), in *Estia*, 18 (1884), pp. 461–7; G. Leidinger, 'Über die Klenzeana der Münchner Staatsbibliotek', in *Jahrbuch der Bildenden Künste*, Munich, 1912; O. Hederer, *Leo von Klenze*, Munich, 1969.

48 Wilhelm von Weiler, *The Central Hospital, Athens*, 1836 (detail)
Watercolour, 50 × 70 cm
Inscribed 'Militair hospital in Athen entworfen und erbaut anno 1836'
National Historical Museum, Athens

Practically nothing is known about the German architect Wilhelm von Weiler, except that he was responsible for the plans of the city of Hermoupolis, in Syros, in 1836.

49 Giorgio Peritelli, *Syntagma (Constitution) Square*, 1863
Oil on canvas, 55 × 76 cm
Private collection, Athens

Very little is known about the Italian artist Giorgio Peritelli. He was invited to Athens in 1863 by Nikolas Argyriou, whose house is depicted in the foreground on the right of the square.

50 Mary Hogarth, *The Athenian Market in Aeolus Street*, c. 1890
Watercolour, 51.5 × 36.5 cm
Private collection, Athens

Mary Hogarth, the sister of the Director of the British School of Archaeology, David Hogarth, visited Athens in about 1890. Soon after, she and her brother published a folio of Greek views enby Mary Hogarth, Described by David Hogarth.

51 Mary Hogarth, *The Church of St Eleutherios, or the Old Cathedral*, c. 1890
Watercolour, 37.5 × 57.5 cm
Private collection, Athens

52 Ludwig Köllnberger, *The Custom House in Piraeus*, 1837
Watercolour, 14.5 × 21.5 cm
National Historical Museum, Athens

53 Joseph Mallord William Turner, *The Temple of Minerva at Sunium*, 1832
From *Finden's Illustrations to Murray's First Complete and Uniform Edition of the Life and Works of Lord Byron*, 17 vols, London, 1832–4
Engraving, 9.5 × 13.5 cm

54 William Henry Bartlett, *The Temple of Minerva at Cape Colonna (Sunium)*, late 1830s (detail)
Watercolour and gouache, 72 × 126 cm
Benaki Museum, Athens

Byron, in one of his notes to *Childe Harold* (Canto II, note 6), wrote that when a visitor sees Cape Colonna 'Pallas and Plato are forgotten in the recollection of Falconer'. William Falconer's *The Shipwreck, a Poem in Three Cantos*, is a description of his experiences during his life at sea and of his shipwreck off Cape Sunium, from which he and two others were the only survivors. The poem was so popular that it went through twelve editions between 1762 and 1800.
William Henry Bartlett (1809–54) visited Greece in the late 1830s on his return from Egypt. Bartlett described his visit to Greece in *Footsteps of Our Lord and His Apostles in Syria, Greece and Italy*, London, 1850, pp. 100–20.

55 Karl Wilhelm von Heydeck, *View of Nafplion*, 1834
From A. Blouet *et al.*, *Expédition scientifique de Morée, ordonnée par le gouvernement français*, Paris, 1831–8
Lithograph, 18 × 51 cm

56 Karl Krazeisen, *View of Fort Palamede at Nafplion*, 1828
From K. Krazeisen, *Bildnisse ausgezeichneter Griechen und Philhellenen nebst einigen Ansichten und Trachten*, Part I, Munich, 1828
Lithograph, 31.5 × 25.5 cm

57 Théodore du Moncel, *View of Mycenae*, c. 1843
From Th. du Moncel, *De Venise à Constantinople à travers la Grèce*, Paris, [1843?], pl. 33
Coloured lithograph, 34 × 50.5 cm

58 Otto Magnus von Stackelberg, *The Lion Gate at Mycenae*, 1812
From O. M. von Stackelberg, *La Grèce. Vues pittoresques et topographiques*, Paris, 1834
Lithograph, 32 × 63 cm

59 Edward Dodwell, *Interior of the Treasury of Atreus*, 1834
From E. Dodwell, *Views and Descriptions of Cyclopian, or, Pelasgic Remains in Greece and Italy; . . . from Drawings by the Late E. Dodwell*, London, 1834

60 William Page, *The Temple of Zeus in Nemea*, 1820
Watercolour, 28 × 40 cm
Private collection, Athens

61 Edward Lear, *View of Sparta from the Ancient Theatre*, 1849/80
Watercolour and gouache, 30 × 51 cm
Signed and dated
The Earl of Derby collection

62 Otto Magnus von Stackelberg, *View of Mistras*, 1812
From O. M. von Stackelberg, *La Grèce. Vues pittoresques et topographiques*, Paris, 1834
Lithograph, 32 × 60 cm

63 Prosper Baccuet, *View of Mistras*, 1831
From A. Blouet *et al.*, *Expédition scientifique de Morée, ordonnée par le gouvernement français*, Paris, 1831–8
Lithograph, 23.5 × 36 cm

Prosper Baccuet (1789–1854) visited Greece in 1830, as a member of the French Scientific Expedition to the Morea.

64 Edward Dodwell, *The Temple of Apollo at Bassae*, 1806
Pencil and watercolour, 23 × 44 cm
Signed, dated 'Feb. 1806', and inscribed 'The mountains covered with wood – small corn plain . . . O. great lens'
Fine Art Society, London

65 Edward Lear, *The Temple of Apollo at Bassae*, 1854/55 (detail)
Oil on canvas, 146.4 × 229.6 cm
Signed in monogram and dated
Fitzwilliam Museum, Cambridge

66 Otto Magnus von Stackelberg, *View of Andritsaina*, 1812
From O. M. von Stackelberg, *La Grèce. Vues pittoresques et topographiques*, Paris, 1834
Lithograph, 26.5 × 39.5 cm

67 Otto Magnus von Stackelberg, *The Bazaar of Corinth*, 1812
From O. M. von Stackelberg, *Trachten und Gebräuche der Neugriechen*, Berlin, 1831
Coloured lithograph, 15 × 22 cm

68 William Cole, *The Temple of Apollo at Corinth*, 1833
From W. Cole, *Select Views of the Remains of Ancient Monuments in Greece*, London, 1835
Coloured aquatint, 22.5 × 30.5 cm

The British architect William Cole visited Attica and the Peloponnesus in 1833. The drawings he made were published as a folio of aquatints, *Select Views of the Remains of Ancient Monuments in Greece as at Present Existing*, London, 1835.
BIBLIOGRAPHY: J. Hemingway, *History of Chester*, London, 1831.

69 Ludwig Lange, *A Dovecote in Tenos*, 1835
Watercolour, 24 × 32 cm
Staatliche Graphische Sammlung, Munich

The German architect Ludwig Lange (1808–68) accompanied Karl Rottmann to Greece in 1834. He stayed in Athens until 1839 as drawing master at the Gymnasium. In 1865 he participated in the competition for the Archaeological Museum in Athens. Lange contributed some illustrations to F. Stademann's *Panorama von Athen* in 1841.
BIBLIOGRAPHY: 'Das neue archäologische Museum für Athen nach dem Projekt von Prof. L. Lange in München', in *Leipziger illustrirte Zeitung*, 45 (14 October 1865), pp. 263–4; Obituary in *Leipziger illustrirte Zeitung*, 50 (2 May 1868), pp. 303–6; C. W. J. Eliot, 'Who Designed the Anglican Church of St Paul in Athens?', in *Polis and Imperium: Studies in Honour of T. Salmon*, Toronto, 1974.

Colour Plates XXIII–XXX (pp. 168–177)

XXIII William Linton, *View of the Town of Arcadia (Kyparissia)*, 1840
Oil on canvas, 27 × 37 cm
Signed and dated, and inscribed 'Arcadian phantasy'
Private collection, Athens

William Linton (1788–1876) made an extensive tour of Greece in 1840. In 1851 he published an illustrated account of his travels entitled *The Scenery of Greece and its Islands*. For an appreciation of Linton's Greek works, see F. M. Tsigakou, 'Edward Lear in Greece', unpublished M. Phil. thesis, University College, London, pp. 58–60.

XXIV Karl Rottmann, *View of the Plain of Olympia with the River Alpheus*, 1835
Watercolour, 21.3 × 29.7 cm
Staatliche Graphische Sammlung, Munich

XXV William Page, *View of Corinth with the Acrocorinthus*, 1820
Watercolour, 28 × 40 cm
Private collection, Athens

XXVI Hugh William Williams, *The Temple of Jupiter Penhellenius (Aphaea) in Aegina* 1820
Watercolour and gouache, 51 × 80 cm
Signed and dated
Private collection, Athens

XXVII Alexandre Gabriel Decamps, *A House in Syros*, c. 1823
Watercolour, 24.5 × 32 cm
Private collection, Athens

Alexandre Gabriel Decamps (1803–60) visited Greece briefly in 1827 with A. L. Garneray.
BIBLIOGRAPHY: D. F. Mosby, 'Alexandre-Gabriel Decamps', Ph.D. thesis, Harvard University, 1973.

XXVIII Karl Rottmann, *View of Santorini with the Volcano*, 1835
Watercolour, 27.7 × 38 cm
Staatliche Graphische Sammlung, Munich

XXIX Edward Lear, *View of Chania, Crete*, 1864
Pen and watercolour, 35 × 53 cm
Inscribed 'Khanea 28 May 1864 5.30–6. P.M. (176) . . . catch gold light grass & asphodel . . . all the distance is very pale blue-gray . . . Stems of olives, indigo, and red, & oker very dark'
Gennadeios Library, Athens

XXX Thomas Hope, *View of Naxos with the Portico of the Temple of Bacchus*, c. 1795
Watercolour, 41.5 × 29 cm
Benaki Museum, Athens

Thomas Hope (1769–1851) visited Greece in c. 1795. He made a large number of drawings and watercolours there, over 300 of which survive in the collection of the Benaki Museum, Athens.
BIBLIOGRAPHY: David Watkin, *Thomas Hope 1769–1831 and the Neo-Classical Idea*, London, 1968, p. 65, n. 11.

Plates 70–78 (pp. 178–185)

70 William James Muller, *View of the Island of Salamis*, 1838
Watercolour, 35 × 55 cm
Benaki Museum, Athens

William James Muller (1812–45) paid a brief visit to Greece in September–October 1838. A large number of his Greek drawings were included in the sales of his works at Christies on 1–3 April 1846, and 1 April 1859.
BIBLIOGRAPHY: N. Neal Solly, *Memoir of the Life of W. J. Müller*, London, 1875; Cyril G. E. Bunt, *The Life and Work of W. J. Müller*, London, 1949.

71 Karl Krazeisen, *View of Aegina*, 1826
From K. Krazeisen, *Bildnisse ausgezeichneter Griechen und Philhellenen nebst einigen Ansichten und Trachten*, Munich, 1828
Lithograph, 25.5 × 31.5 cm

72 Thomas Hope, *View of the Town and Harbour of Hydra*, c. 1795
Sepia drawing, 19 × 29 cm
Benaki Museum, Athens

73 Wilhelm von Weiler, *View of Poros with the Monastery of Phaneromeni*, 1836
Watercolour, 52 × 65 cm
Benaki Museum, Athens

74 Thomas Hope, *View of the Island and Town of Tenos*, c. 1795
Sepia drawing, 26 × 43 cm
Benaki Museum, Athens

75 James Skene, *View of Melos with the Monastery of St Marina*, 1841
Watercolour, 50 × 40 cm
Inscribed 'S' Marina Monastry. island of Milo 30 June 1841.'
British Museum, London

76 William Gell, *View of the Monastery of Nea Moni in Chios*, 1801
Pen drawing, 27 × 52 cm
British Museum, London

77 William James Muller, *View of the Port of Rhodes*, 1838
Watercolour, 25 × 35 cm
Inscribed 'The Pasha's Palace Rhodes'
Museum of the City of Athens

78 P. J. Witdoeck, *View of the Street of the Knights, Rhodes*, 1825
From *Monumens de Rhodes*, Brussels, 1828
Lithograph, 30 × 22.5 cm

The illustrated folio *Monumens de Rhodes* was issued to complement Colonel Bernard Rottiers's *Description des monumens de Rhodes* (Brussels, 1830). Both publications were the result of a Dutch archaeological expedition to the Aegean in 1825, led by Rottiers and under the auspices of the King of the Netherlands. The Dutch draughtsman P. J. Witdoeck (1803–40) seems to have accompanied the expedition.

Index